Woman in
the Case

CHARLES FRANKLIN

Usher, Frank Hugh

Woman in the Case

Illustrated

TAPLINGER PUBLISHING COMPANY
New York

First published in the United States in 1968 by
TAPLINGER PUBLISHING CO., INC.
29 East Tenth Street
New York, New York 10003

345.02523   *Us3w*
c.1

Copyright © Charles Franklin 1963 and 1967

Library of Congress Catalog Card Number 68-12697

PRINTED IN GREAT BRITAIN

CONTENTS

" I have hated only one person in my life and I have proved the strength of my hatred." Charlotte Corday (1793)

" If there is an after life, it would be a dirty trick." Starr Faithfull (1931)

" Don't let them kill me on Wednesday . . ." Charlotte Bryant's appeal to Edward VIII (1936)

ILLUSTRATIONS

INTRODUCTION

THIS BOOK contains word sketches of nine women who have been involved in criminal cases. Only three of them are murderesses, but each of the others played a vital part in a crime. The people lurking in the wings are often more interesting than the criminal who takes the full limelight. In every interesting crime there is somewhere a woman.

Here are nine women. You may not have heard of some of them, but each has left her mark on the annals of crime. They are Charlotte Corday, Gay Gibson, Starr Faithfull, Marguerite Diblanc, Jeanette Edmonds, Ellen Turner, Judith Morton, Charlotte Bryant and Valerie Storie.

A woman like Judith Morton, who got her men to do her murders for her, and who was never, so far as we know, accused of any crime, deserves as much attention as the Madeleine Smiths and Alma Rattenburys. The formidable, and they said very attractive, Jeanette Edmonds, deserves a certain fame for provoking one of the most fascinating mid-Victorian murder trials, that of her uncle, even if her only crime was an unashamed immorality. A serious business, of course, in her day, but perhaps she had been reading about Victoria Woodhull, who in that very year was scandalising New York with her bold affirmation that she was a practising free-lover.

Charlotte Corday is certainly worth looking at again. Viewed 170 years later, opinion has changed a little about this glamorous assassin of the French Revolution. She is perhaps as inter-

9

esting subject for Freudian study as that other strange sister of hers, Joan of Arc. But to her contemporaries Charlotte Corday was a creature compounded of all that was good and lovely, in whom dwelt some strange and terrible force. The effect of her death, wrote Jules Michelet, was to make death more beautiful. Young men committed suicide because of her. André Chénier wrote a hymn to her. So did the Russian poet Pushkin, author of *Eugène Onegin*. She inspired his *Hymn to the Poniard*. What does this remarkable young woman inspire in us today?

The sad story of Gay Gibson deserves telling again, with perhaps a little more understanding of the behaviour of this unfortunate girl, whose death on a homeward-bound Union Castle liner in 1947 firmly established the fact that a murder charge can be successfully proved without a body.

Starr Faithfull, that fascinating enigma of the Charleston age, has been so much fictionalised that the known facts of her story are likely to be forgotten.

As for Valerie Storie, she certainly deserves a place in a collection of this kind, for her story of terror and heroism is typical of this sick age of purposeless crime. There is for me one unforgettable moment during that night at the lay-by at Dead Man's Hill, when after the gunman had shot Gregsten and then raped her, she gave him a pound note to persuade him to go away then and leave her with her dead. Was it for this splendid gesture of despairing contempt that he crowned his bestial outrage by shooting her too?

Two of these cases—Judith Morton and Jeanette Edmonds—have been used by me as the basis for radio plays, but there is, I believe, an element of drama and humanity in each of the stories told in this book.

CHARLES FRANKLIN

Charlotte Corday
(1793)

CHARLOTTE CORDAY runs Joan of Arc a close second for being the most romanticised female in French history.

The English have romanticised her even more than the French, and Victorian ladies like Julia Kavanagh, Jeanette van Alstine and Mary Jeaffreson wrote an abundance of fulsome prose about the chaste young aristocrat from Normandy who went to Paris in that hot and bloody July of 1793 and stuck a carving knife into the heart of Jean-Paul Marat as he lay in his bath, and then with a splendid and cold-blooded indifference to death, rode in the tumbril to the guillotine in the middle of a spectacular thunderstorm.

What more could the English want? A pure avenging virgin who came from a good family. Even the heavens were kind and provided a suitable meteorological send-off. Surely this was evidence of Divine approval.

None of her biographers is prepared to admit that she committed a stupid and ignorant murder which had harmful consequences for France. To them Marat was a foul and hideous monster, a bloodthirsty tyrant, slain by the hand of a brave, beautiful and virtuous girl.

The black-and-white world was all right for the Victorians, and seemed to hold good until the thirties for some people. The Baroness Orczy view of the French Revolution was a long time dying.

The last serious study of Charlotte Corday to be published in

England was in 1935. It was Joseph Shearing's *The Angel of the Assassination*.* Mr. Shearing maintained the same Beauty-and-the-Beast approach which makes most of the English-written Corday literature rather starry-eyed and naïve. Purporting also to tell the story of Adam Lux, it failed to mention the following vital judgement which this tragic young German made on Charlotte Corday : " No doubt one has a right to kill a usurper or a tyrant. But Marat was neither."

It was Lamartine who called her *L'ange de l'assassinat*. In 1793 she had an electrifying effect upon a Paris tormented, bleeding, confused, torn with darkness, violence and horror. She was the brightest star that flamed across the stormy skies in those awful and thrilling years, making Louis and his queen look like vulgar martyrs.

No wonder she shook Revolutionary Paris to its foundations, that a new religion was born of her blood—the Religion of the Poniard, that she became the Patroness of Heroic Murder, the saint with the knife, a new divinity more powerful, more seductive than the pale memory of Brutus.

One of her contemporary worshippers wrote of her : " O Charlotte Corday, thou wilt always appear before our eyes superb and gentle, modest and beautiful, as thou wert with thy bearing, full of dignified assurance, thy glance of fire tempered by sweetness. Charlotte Corday, thou who wilt ever be the idol of the Republicans in the Elysium where thy repose is shared by Vergniant, Sidney and Brutus, hear my last vows!"

This fanaticism was excusable in men who saw her and knew her in those wild distracted days when the new France was being born in blood and confusion. But they did not entirely lose their sense of proportion. It was the latter-day Corday worshippers who did that.

What sort of person was this Charlotte Corday, who with her terrible purity and tragic voluptuousness turned the very guillotine into an altar on that memorable evening of 17th July 1793? This " celestial being for whom the earth was unfit ".

One has only to read her life and her last letters to realise that

* Heinemann.

here was an unusual girl, with intelligence, personality, wit, independence, an inflexible determination and remarkable courage in the face of death. After an intensive study of the classics, she had completely acquired the ancient Stoics' indifference to death. More than that, she welcomed death. And with this death wish—something she shared with that other strange sister of hers, Starr Faithfull—she combined an exaggerated fear of any infringement of her modesty.

There is something else about her which is important to any understanding of this remarkable girl—her solitude. " She had always been alone," said Michelet, writing in 1854. " There lurked in her that sinister power, the demon of solitude. This perhaps explains her whole destiny."

She also had a strong desire to be a saint and a martyr, to be immortal, to be remembered, to be the heroine dying for her country. These traits are not the most desirable in a young girl, and those who don't grow out of them might be said to have delusions of grandeur. The fact that Charlotte Corday was able to realise her dreams and create the extraordinary impression she did is more a tribute to the vividness of her person—and her personality—than to the rightness of her motives, or her cause.

She was born into a noble but impoverished Norman family, and, against a background of genteel poverty, she was never allowed to forget her noble birth.

During her childhood, both at home and at school, she was continually in trouble on account of her independent spirit. The dramatist Corneille was her great-uncle and she had a superstitious reverence for his works. From these heroic plays, she imbibed the virtues and the strength of ancient Sparta. This was not unusual, for that was the spirit of those days. As during the Renaissance, there was a great revival of the cult of antiquity at the end of the eighteenth century. The Girondins, for whose cause Charlotte Corday killed Marat, cultivated an exaggerated worship of ancient Rome.

Her mother died while she was a child and her father took little interest in his children and was concerned more with the ruinous state of France at the end of the *ancien régime*. He

13

put Charlotte into the Abbaye-aux-Dames, a convent for the daughters of impoverished nobility at Caen.

The chaste life of the convent school where she combined a study of the lives of the saints with the exploits of the ancient heroes, undoubtedly did much to fashion her into the avenging virgin of July, 1793.

But the tremendous events of 1789 were felt even in the sleepy little town of Caen, when it experienced a sudden and savage wave of revolutionary violence which washed even up to the cloistered walls of the Abbaye.

The nephew of the Abbess, Vicomte Henri de Belzunce, a haughty and brash young army officer, enraged the local mob by his insolence and, inspired by what had been happening in Paris, the mob turned on him and tore him to pieces. One cut open his chest and plucked out his heart. A young plasterer, his arms covered up to the elbows with blood, threw the warm ball into the air.

A woman caught it, they said, and after sticking the still-palpitating flesh on a red-hot spike, ate it. Others cut off the head and tore out the entrails and, hoisting them on pitchforks, marched round the town with them to the beat of drums. The procession halted at a hairdresser's to have the hair on the head curled. Farther on, when it had been spat upon and subjected to unmentionable indignities, the mob forced passers-by whom they considered too well-dressed to kiss it. Finally they took the hideous remains to the windows of the Abbaye-aux-Dames.

Thus the Revolution came to Caen, and its ugliest side was seen for the first time by Charlotte Corday.

In 1791 she left the Abbaye. Her father had married again and she went to live with her aunt, Madame Breteville, in Caen. Here, Charlotte, a confirmed Republican, took an intense interest in the progress of the Revolution which was shaking to its foundations not only France but all Europe as well.

Here she lived until she set off to Paris on her sacred mission of murder.

She gave her passionate allegiance to the Girondins, and it was on their behalf that she struck down their mortal enemy, Jean-Paul Marat.

The Girondins were about the most inept of the ruling factions which battled for power in Revolutionary Paris. A middle-class party, they were anti-democratic. They did not want the people to have any power, and they wanted to decentralise the government from Paris. They made use of democracy, but despised it, and by 1792 were thoroughly discredited in the eyes of the country.

It was said that the Girondins failed to excite the enthusiasm of anyone, save Charlotte Corday, who by killing Marat, set the seal on their doom. The Girondins were distinguished by their wit, elegance, fine rhetoric and devotion to antiquity. It is easy to see what attracted Charlotte Corday to their cause.

When the Girondins fell in Paris, they spread to the provinces and tried to raise the country against the capital. They came to Caen to recruit a force of volunteers to march on Paris to fight what they called the Marat War. But they did not fire the enthusiasm of the local men, and barely thirty volunteered, mostly ne'er-do-wells. The fair ladies and deputies of Caen who assembled to see the volunteers parade on 7th July 1793, were surprised and chagrined at the meagreness of their number.

Charlotte Corday was there on that green field of Mars that hot summer's day, and was most aggrieved of all. She had already conceived a great hatred for Marat. Thoughts of murder were burning deep down in the far-from-innocent heart of this cultured girl, whose bright beauty and vivid personality were the talk of Caen.

And while the deputies argued, the drums rolled and the armed men marched outside in the hot streets, the Angel Assassin sat in her aunt's cool, sunless house, calmly contemplating, as she plied her needle, whether or whether not to do the terrible thing which she believed she was born into the world to do.

On a piece of silk she had embroidered the words which haunted her mind continually: *Le ferai-je? Ne le ferai-je?*— Shall I? Shall I not?

Who was this man Marat who had incurred the hatred of the Girondins and their avenging angel?

Jean-Paul Marat was a man of commanding and clear-sighted intelligence, and was perhaps the greatest leader produced by the Revolution. He was a brilliant scientist who had turned politician. He had spent some years in England and was an honorary M.D. of St. Andrew's. He had published some valuable contributions to medical science. His experimental work in physics aroused the interest of men like Benjamin Franklin and Goethe.

In the 1770's he became famous in European medical and scientific circles, and his views on heat, light and electricity caused a sensation because he dared to challenge the ideas of Newton.

At the outbreak of the Revolution he threw himself into politics, wrote several arresting pamphlets and started his famous paper *L'Ami du Peuple*.

Always he stood alone. He never attached himself to any party. He suspected whoever was in power, and with good reason. He attacked the most powerful factions in Paris, had to flee to England to escape arrest, and spent months hiding in the cellars and sewers of Paris where he caught a painful skin disease, the agonies of which he could only ease by sitting in his bath.

Marat was unpopular in the Assembly, though the people loved him. He was not the tyrant or sadist which Carlyle portrayed. He had no lust for power. His only power lay in his fiery eloquence in the Assembly and his great hold on the people. He always suspected and opposed the powerful, and refused power himself.

He was the only man in France who could and would have opposed and checked Robespierre, whose government of blood and terror followed the brief visit of the Angel Assassin to Paris, and may be said to have been one of the consequences of it. With Marat, the people's terrible friend, out of the way, Robespierre was safe to set up the Terror.

Poor Charlotte Corday! She could not have dreamed what suffering she unwittingly brought upon the good people of Paris. She believed that, like Joan of Arc, she was born to save France. In killing Marat, she didn't really know what she was doing.

Marat's integrity and great sense of justice was demonstrated during the trial of Louis XVI. Though he was implacable in his hostility to the king, he held that it was unfair to accuse him of anything which happened before his acceptance of the Constitution, and he would not allow Louis' counsel to be attacked in his paper.

When the Girondins fell, they blamed Marat, although Marat had the people behind him. The Girondins who fled to Caen represented Marat as a tyrant. But it was they, not Marat, who despised the people.

Charlotte Corday no doubt thought their words were divinely inspired. It is not likely that she had more than a hazy idea of the political situation in France. The Girondins say Marat is a tyrant. Tyrants should not be allowed to live in France. Therefore she was ordained to slay the tyrant. She was, in fact, just another woman who meddled in politics, and made things very much worse as a consequence. There are many such women throughout history. Some of these women, of course, had a good effect upon the course of events. But Charlotte Corday was not one of these.

What was she really like, this twenty-five-year-old Norman beauty who has bewitched us for a century and a half?

Nowadays we take a very much cooler view of this knife-wielding enchantress.

Of her beauty there is overwhelming oral and written evidence. But judging by the only genuine portrait of her which has come down to us, her beauty was exaggerated.

The artist concerned, Jean Jacques Hauer, was not in the best tradition of French portraitists. His picture, which he painted while she was waiting to be taken to her death, is at Versailles, and lacks both character and style.

He appears to have fallen utterly under her spell, and was completely overcome. He could hardly paint for his tears, so he may not have been at his best, though one might have reasonably expected that the poignancy of the situation and the electrifying drama of her death would have inspired him to have painted something really great on the basis of his death-cell sketch.

Hauer's portrait does not capture this elusive, legendary beauty of Charlotte Corday which seemed to have haunted everybody who saw her.

Those who testified to her beauty did so after her death—

after she had become the legend—when to have known her, or even seen her, was fame. So perhaps a little exaggeration was pardonable.

According to her passport, which is still preserved, she was five feet one inch, with chestnut-coloured hair, grey eyes, high forehead, a long nose, a mouth of medium size, and an oval face with a round, cleft chin.

This description does not quite tally with many descriptions given by those who saw her. For instance, many said she was tall, but this discrepancy has been explained by the suggestion that in the passport measurement of her height, *cinq pieds, un pouce*, the *pouce* was the old inch measurement which was considerably more than the modern inch.

Again, her hair has been variously described as fair, reddish-gold, and even ash-blonde. This might be explained by the habit ladies had in those days of powdering their hair.

She certainly had a long nose and a prominent chin. That is plain from Hauer's portrait. But this does not necessarily detract from an overall attraction. One woman who knew her in Caen said of her later that she did not hold herself well. " Her head always drooped a little." But this witness said she was tall and very beautiful, with a well formed, if somewhat robust figure, with deep-set, beautiful eyes, whose expression was slightly veiled, and with a tendency to blush easily—one of maidenhood's most attractive assets in those days.

There is little doubt that she was a very attractive and noticeable girl with a magnetic personality and an unusually melodious voice. Even her enemies gave her this.

On July 9th, 1793, she wrote the following letter to her father :

I owe you obedience, my dear papa, yet I am leaving without your permission, without seeing you, because I am too full of grief, I am going to England because I do not believe that one can at present live for very long happy and tranquil in France. In leaving, I put this letter in the post for you and when you receive it I shall no longer be in this country. Heaven refuses us the happiness of living together as it has denied us so many other blessings. Perhaps it will be more clement towards our country. Farewell, my dear papa, embrace my sister for me, and do not forget me.

Corday.

She went to sleep that night thinking of the words of Barbaroux, a young Girondin who had inspired her with his eloquence : " Without another Jeanne d'Arc, without some deliverer sent from heaven, without some unexpected miracle, what is to become of France?"

The next morning the self-appointed deliverer said her modest farewells and boarded the coach for Paris. She had hardly any luggage with her and very little money. She in fact correctly gauged her worldly requirements to last her for the few more days she had to live.

The heat wave continued and the diligence rolled out of Caen, whose old stone buildings shimmered in the heat haze.

What were the thoughts veiled behind those fine, deep-set eyes as the stuffy coach rocked along the road to Paris, with the other passengers speculatively eyeing this curiously attractive girl who seemed quite out of place in their midst?

She knew she had left Normandy for ever, and she almost certainly knew she was going to her death. But what had decided her to do this thing?

She explained it in an extraordinary letter she wrote while she was in prison awaiting certain death. This highly revealing letter is the best clue there is to the character of this strange girl. It is addressed to Barbaroux—though she knew well enough he would never receive it—and in it she says: " I confess that what finally decided me was the courage with which our volunteers enlisted on 7th of July. You remember how charmed I was, and I promised myself that I would make Pétion regret the suspicions he harboured with regard to my feelings. ' Would you be sorry if they did not go?' he asked me. In short, I came to the conclusion that it was foolish for so many brave men to try for the head of one man whom they might miss or who might drag down a number of worthy citizens with him. He did not

19

deserve the honour. A woman's hand was enough!'"

Her intention was clear. She knew what she was about and she performed the job with the efficiency and despatch of the professional killer. She was not, of course, that. But to murder a complete stranger in cold blood requires a very special sort of nerve and mentality which has nothing to do with any kind of religious dedication. She was one of the coolest, most efficient and fearless killers in history, and she showed little of the sort of fanaticism which one might have expected in view of the circumstances.

But before she got to Paris there was a little romantic interlude in the diligence which obviously appealed to her charming sense of humour. Let her tell it in her own words, remembering that this was written by this astonishing girl under the very shadow of the guillotine with that appalling death ride a matter of a few hours away.

"I travelled with good Montagnards whom I allowed to chatter to their hearts' content, and as their conversation was as stupid as their persons were disagreeable, I found it all the easier to go to sleep. I might say I woke up only on reaching Paris.

"One of my travelling companions who doubtless likes women when they are asleep, thought I was the daughter of an old friend of his. He endowed me with a fortune I do not possess, gave me a name which I have never heard, and in the end offered me his hand with all his worldly goods. 'We are playing a regular comedy,' I said when I began to grow tired of his attentions. 'It is unfortunate that so much talent should not have an audience. I am going to fetch our fellow-travellers so that they may share the entertainment.' And in a very bad temper he left me. During the night he murmured plaintive ditties which were extremely soporific in their effect. At last when we reached Paris, I got rid of him, refusing to give him either my own or my father's address. He wanted to ask my father for my hand. He was very cross when he left me."

And so, dismissing all thoughts of natural things like romance from her mind, she arrived in Paris, this gentle girl with murder in her ungentle heart.

She engaged a room at the Hôtel de la Providence in the rue des Vieux-Augustins. The first thing she did was to discharge a debt of friendship which was the pretext for her journey to Paris. At Caen she had obtained a letter from Barbaroux to his colleague Deperret. She had declared that she wanted to use Deperret's influence to get certain documents from the Ministry of the Interior necessary to an emigrée friend of hers.

She went to see Deperret, a wealthy Girondin, who had escaped arrest on account of his moderation. She wanted to get into the Convention and kill Marat there. He saw her for a brief while at his home and then the following day took her to the Ministry, but the Minister refused to see either of them as he did not wish to compromise himself with a Girondin. Everyone was scared in Paris those days.

Deperret and Charlotte Corday did not meet again. But this slight contact with her was sufficient to cost Deperret his head. To have had any contact with her then meant death.

Learning that Marat was ill and confined to his house, she determined to go there and do the deed.

On the morning of the 13th she went out early. It was another hot sunny day. She bought a kitchen knife in a cutler's shop in the Palais Royal—then called Palais Égalité. She selected it with care. It had a flexible blade about six inches long, with an ebony handle and a shagreen sheath. Fresh from the grinding stone, it was razor-sharp. She hid the knife in her bodice.

About nine o'clock she hired a fiacre and told the driver to take her to Marat's house. It took him some time to find where Marat lived and they eventually came to No. 20, rue des Cordeliers.

In this house Marat lived with his mistress, Simonne Evrard, and her sister Albertine, who was away at the time. Both these women were devoted to him.

Marat, though he was born in Neuchâtel, was a Mediterranean, his father being a Sardinian. He was supposed to have been a very ugly man. According to his enemies he had dirty and offensive habits. No doubt Marat's looks were deliberately disparaged in the same way as Charlotte Corday's were over-praised. It's the old idea of Beauty and the Beast which always has great appeal.

There are a number of portraits of Marat—one painted in the year of his death by Joseph Boze showing a strong, bold Latin face, with an aquiline nose, a full mouth, high cheek-bones, and intelligent eyes. Certainly the face of a leader, even an intellectual. And Marat unquestionably was an intellectual.

So was the girl who was now closing in to kill him. If ill-assorted, they were well matched.

Charlotte Corday rang the front-door bell. It was answered by Catherine Evrard, the sister of Simonne. She told this fine young lady with the soft Normandy accent that Marat was sick and could see no one.

When Charlotte persisted and asked when it would be possible to see him, Simonne appeared and told her that no one could say when Marat would be well enough to see anyone. It was useless for her to call again.

Repulsed, but by no means discouraged, Charlotte returned to her hotel to plan her next move. She wrote Marat a letter which said:

" I come from Caen. Your love of your country must make you wish to know the plots that are hatching there. I await your reply.
              Charlotte de Corday, Hôtel de la Providence."

She went out and posted the letter and was told that it would be delivered in a few hours. The Revolution obviously had not dislocated the postal service of Paris.

She returned to the hotel and stayed in her room until seven in the evening thinking thoughts and even enduring torments which will never be known.

Then she dressed herself in her most elegant clothes and left for the encounter with death. She put on a gown of spotted Indian muslin over a grey underskirt, and covered her shoulders with a rose-coloured scarf or fichu of the most delicate gauze. She wore a tall hat with a black cockade and green ribbons on her delicately powdered hair. She carried gloves and a fan.

What sort of girl was this, we ask in the far from innocent 1960's, who would dress herself in her most beautiful clothes to go and commit a murder? This was going to be no stab in a dark alley. She was not going to lure him to a safe place where she could despatch him at her convenience. She was no siren who was going to knife him under the pretence of seduction. In fact, if he had made a pass at her she would probably have thrown up the whole thing and fled in horror. An assault on her precious modesty was the only thing this extraordinary girl was afraid of.

Her plan was to walk boldly into his house in the face of his servants and his suspiciously protective mistress, and kill him practically in front of them. Was there ever such a bold and audacious murder? Did ever a killer challenge such odds? It is true, of course, that she did not care whether or not she died in the attempt. In fact she expected and desired death. But first her bold plan had to succeed.

It is even more astonishing that her daring plan did succeed. There was more than luck in this. She just made it succeed, this gentle murderess from Normandy, with her deadly determination and inflexible will.

The astonishing thing is that she was so confident that it would succeed. Perhaps her very innocence gave her this confidence.

Once more she took the fiacre to 20, rue des Cordeliers, where she arrived at seven o'clock.

The bottom part of the house was occupied by Marat's printing press. The latest issue of *L'Ami du Peuple* was hot off the press and the place was busy with people working on the packing and distribution. This issue, No. 242, dated 14th July, 1793, was the very last one, for the paper died with Marat, the Friend of the People.

Telling the driver of the fiacre to wait, Charlotte Corday went into the courtyard and rang the bell of Marat's door. It was opened by Marat's cook. Behind her was the concierge, busy folding papers.

Again she was refused admission. She now argued vigorously saying she had important and vital business with Citizen Marat.

Had he not received her letter? The argument attracted Simonne Evrard, who said that perhaps Marat could see her in a few days' time.

Marat himself, hearing the disturbance, called out to ask what it was. Simonne went in to tell him and presently came out saying that Marat would see the citizeness from Caen, whose letter he had just received.

Simonne was about the same age as Charlotte, and was not unattractive. She was not the slattern Marat's detractors made out, but was an intelligent, respectable young woman with means of her own, who loved and cared for this strange and remarkable man with great devotion. He was twice her age and suffered terribly from the painful skin disease he had contracted while hiding in the sewers. He was not an attractive sight.

Simonne conducted Charlotte to a small bathroom adjoining the bedroom.

Marat was seated in a slipper bath made of copper. A board laid across the bath was covered with papers and newspapers and at his side was an inkstand on a wooden block. On the wall was a map of France, and under it a shelf on which was a pair of pistols.

A dressing-gown was around his shoulders. Underneath it he was naked, though the board and the shape of the bath concealed his body.

For a man to receive strange young ladies while he was in his bath would be considered highly unconventional, even scandalous in these free and easy times. And yet Charlotte Corday, with her virginal upbringing and strictly puritan outlook, did not appear to have been shocked. Perhaps she was so overwhelmed at finally having got into his presence.

It seems there was some conversation. At first she hesitated to strike, and made out she had come there to betray the Girondins to him. He asked about the state of affairs at Caen.

Then Simonne Evrard came into the room on some pretext about his medicine. Did she have some presentiment that something was wrong, some forewarning of the disaster? She was certainly on edge.

Charlotte Corday knew that time and opportunity were slipping by. Marat continued to ask questions. Simonne left the room with two dishes which had been placed on the window-sill for the evening meal.

Marat asked for the names of the deputies who were rousing the countryside against the capital. Charlotte told him—Pétion, Louvet, Gaudet, Buzot and Barbaroux.

He assured her that they would be guillotined.

Now this was not, as has been suggested, the boast of a blood-thirsty tyrant. France was then at war. The Allies were attacking her eastern frontiers. Her young men were fighting to defend their country while these Girondins were starting an armed in-surrection at home. If such a thing had happened during World War II in England, the culprits would have been regarded as the basest traitors and hanged. Charlotte Corday's friends de-served death by the standards of the day—and by the standards of today also.

But the Angel Assassin had heard enough. She had heard the very words from the monster's lips. And time was slipping by. She heard the women talking in whispers outside in the passage as they busily folded the last number of *L'Ami du Peuple*. Simonne was at the very door, listening, all suspicion.

The friend of the people bent over his writing board, pen in hand, writing down the names Charlotte Corday had given him, the dressing-gown falling off his shoulders.

She suddenly came over to him, drawing the sheathed knife from her bosom. He may not even have looked up as her shadow fell across the bath.

With a quick movement, she pulled off the shagreen scabbard and then with a sudden downward sweep of her arm, she plunged the knife into his breast up to the hilt.

There was instant uproar and confusion. Simonne burst into the room as Marat fell back into the bath with a terrible cry, his blood crimsoning the steamy water.

With one burning look at Corday, Simonne rushed to her dying lover, crying with horror and grief and tried to pull him out of the bath.

The two other women outside were already screaming " Help! Murder!" as Charlotte Corday ran into the bedroom and then

25

into the salon in an attempt to get away from this terrible scene of death.

The cook, Maréchal, helped Simonne lift Marat out of the bath, and carry him in a trail of blood and water into the bedroom and on to the bed. They were half hysterical. But no sound came from Marat.

The commissionaire, who had also been folding newspapers, rushed into the salon and, picking up a chair, attacked Charlotte Corday with it and knocked her down. As she tried to get up, he knocked her down again, roughly, with his hands, hitting her, swearing at her. Another man joined him and together they secured her, binding her wrists tightly behind her back.

The news spread with great rapidity. An angry crowd gathered, Marat's great popularity was no myth.

A surgeon who lived in the house came in and, clearing the hysterical women out of the bedroom, tried to do something for the stricken man. But it was useless.

Marat was dead.

Charlotte Corday, bound and guarded, heard the words and closed her eyes with thankfulness. Her great mission was completed.

Now what was to happen to her? Death she would welcome. But what would happen first? What would they do to her? Perhaps for the first time she realised how much her deed had infuriated and outraged the people.

Death was nothing to her. Only one thing she dreaded—violation, however slight, of her modesty. How could she avoid that, when the mob were already screaming for her blood, demanding that she should be delivered to them to tear into pieces?

No wonder Corday paled. She was thankful to see two armed members of the National Guard shoulder their way through the crowd and stand guard over her.

Two doctors and Guellard, the local police chief, soon arrived. They examined the scene of the crime—there was blood everywhere—and also the body which lay in an ever-spreading stain on the bed, with the heartbroken Simonne weeping over it, inconsolable, in the uttermost despair. She herself was heavily stained with her lover's blood, for she had tried to staunch the

26

gushing wound in his breast with her own hands.

The doctors informed Guellard that a clean, skilful blow had caused death, which had been as instantaneous as that given by the guillotine. " The knife penetrating the clavicle on the right side between the first and second ribs, traversed the lung, and opened the heart, which accounts for the blood which left the wound in torrents."

Guellard immediately despatched a messenger to the Committee of Public Safety with the news. Then he left the room of death and the desperately weeping Simonne, and went to examine the extraordinary girl who had dared to walk into the lion's den and kill the friend of the people—who were now howling for her blood at the very door.

Guellard found the two guards protecting their prisoner. They were holding back a mob of infuriated women with their pikes. Guellard ordered the mob back, telling them that if the prisoner was punished on the spot, they would never discover who were her fellow conspirators. The people saw the sense of this, and Charlotte's life was saved.

She thanked him for his action and paid a tribute to the bravery of the police.

As for him, he was astonished to find that the assassin was a girl of such extraordinary quality.

She was calm now that the hideous danger of lynching was over. The thing that distressed her was the broken-hearted weeping of Simonne in the next room. She had not reckoned on anyone loving Marat like this, or that her act would cause such terrible distress.

It was now past eight. The candles were lit and Guellard started questioning her.

She had little to say. She explained who she was and said she came to Paris, where she knew no one, to kill Marat. No one prompted her. She had no accomplices.

Guellard did not accept this last statement. She was searched. In her pocket was a gold watch, a key, a silver thimble, a reel of white cotton, a needle, the sheath of the knife, and inside her rose fichu was her certificate of baptism.

Guellard was puzzled and baffled. Who was she, this strangely attractive enigma of a girl, intelligent, educated, with a remarkable personality, and totally unafraid? She knew she was for the guillotine, and that grim knowledge did not disturb her in the least.

In the other room, to the sound of the weeping, the doctors were at work on Marat's body. They were making immediate preparations to embalm him. The pungent odours of the aromatics seeped into the salon where Charlotte Corday sat bound under the questioning of the police chief.

Meanwhile the news was spreading like wildfire through Paris. The authorities were already busy. Police had been sent post-haste through the hot night to the Hôtel de la Providence, and to the offices of the Norman diligence.

Her room was searched, Lauze Deperret's name found, and Deperret was immediately arrested. The hotel staff were all rigorously questioned. The police wanted to know everything that she had done. Travellers on the Norman diligence were rounded up.

A thrill of fear and excitement ran through Paris as the warm night fell. People gathered in the lantern gleams. *Marat est mort—assassiné!* The cry echoed through the streets. The people's friend was dead, and everybody knew that a lot more heads would fall in consequence.

The Committee of Public Safety sent four members of the Convention to Marat's house to examine the assassin. They were Legendre, Maure, Drout and Chabot.

When they saw her they stared at her in astonishment. She was sitting quite still with her hands tied behind her back, guarded by the men with pikes. She had been there in that cramped position for hours. Her wrists had been bound very tightly and she was in considerable discomfort. Her dress was torn and she was bruised from the beating she had received at the hands of the commissionaire. She had been continually insulted and threatened by the mob, and had been sternly questioned by Guellard.

The crowded room was now ablaze with candles and was uncomfortably stuffy. The air was heavy with the smell of burning aromatics and embalming lotions from the adjoining room of death.

In the middle of this the girl assassin sat with an air of serene self-possession which astonished the deputies. Her calmness, her beauty and personality dominated the room.

Beside her on the table were the modest possessions which had been found on her person. She was completely unarmed and harmless, surrounded by armed men, police and deputies, yet they kept her hands tightly bound.

François Chabot, who was an unfrocked priest and a friend of Marat, took charge of the questioning. She replied to him with an arrogance and courage which astonished them all.

" How was it that you were able to strike him to the heart at one blow? You must be well practised."

" The anger in my own heart showed me the way to his," was her quick, uncompromising reply.

For every question she had an answer. This scornful, spirited girl was a match for them all.

Reporters had come into the room and were taking notes of the questioning—men who were no friends or admirers of hers —and on their testimony this scene has gone down in history.

One of them wrote: " She has the gentleness of a cat which offers a velvet paw in order to scratch better. She appears no more troubled than if she had just performed some good deed. She went to prison as coolly as though she was going to a ball."

Did they enjoy tormenting this girl, these deputies who had already made up their minds that she was to die? There is some evidence that Chabot, the ex-priest, did.

It is not surprising that she aroused a kind of sadistic sexual desire. There was something voluptuous about this attractive virginal creature. All those who saw her gave evidence to this. She was no cold virgin. She was well shaped, and that veiled strangeness in her deep-set eyes would make men think of love, not death and murder, which were the only things in her heart. Now she had accomplished what she believed she had been born into the world to do, she wished only for death.

The questioning was nearly over, but Chabot did not want to let her go. He stood over her, looking down at her bosom, full of hate and desire, and spotted a piece of paper which was inside her bodice.

He suddenly thrust his hand right in between her breasts and plucked the paper out.

Charlotte Corday was prepared for death, but to her this indecent hand touching her was worse than death. She leaped to her feet with blazing eyes, and unable to protect herself because of her bound wrists, made a backward movement against the wall so violent that it broke the laces of her bodice.

As the bodice burst apart, her firm full breasts were revealed for a second for all in the room to see. Then she collapsed on the chair, bending double to hide her nakedness, flushing hotly in an agony of shame.

There was utter silence in the room. Then she spoke—her voice, a minute ago fearless and scornful, now low and humble.

"Gentlemen, I beg you—untie my hands and let me adjust my dress."

Chabot turned away a little sheepishly, the paper in his hand. Drouet sharply ordered that her hands be untied.

There was another silence during which she half-turned to the wall on her chair and adjusted her dress, knotting the broken laces as best she could, and covering her torn dress with her now ragged fichu.

Chabot found that the paper hidden in her bosom was merely a newspaper cutting containing an account of the fall of the Girondins.

A deposition had been made out and, as her hands were free, she was told to sign it. She did so, after making several corrections.

As the guard approached to tie her hands again, she took a step towards the deputies and showed them her bare wrists which were red and lacerated by the tightness of her bonds.

"Gentlemen," she said, "if you would be so good as to save me suffering before you put me to death, I beg you to allow me to pull down my sleeves and put on my gloves under the cords."

She knew the reporters were there taking down every word she said—reporters who had no desire to make her into a martyr. Charlotte Corday knew the road to immortality all right.

Her request was, of course, granted, and the cord was tied less tightly. She was after all dealing with Frenchmen and human beings, even though she herself may not have thought they were much above the level of animals. But Charlotte Corday was wrong about a lot of things. She never discovered the magnificent futility of what she was doing.

They took her into the bedroom where the air was heavy with the fumes of the burning pastilles and the body of her victim lay on the bed. When they showed her the gaping wound in his chest, she recoiled.

" Yes, yes—I killed him," she said faintly.

At the foot of the bed Simonne wept and wept, and the deputies keenly watching Charlotte's reaction, saw that though she had no remorse for what she had done, she was distressed at Simonne's desperate grief.

And so they finally took her away. It was well past midnight. The street was crowded with a mob howling for her blood.

Again she faced the danger of being lynched. As soon as she appeared with Drouet and Chabot and surrounded by police, a great baying cry went up.

She hesitated as she appeared in the doorway and paled, but the guards pushed her forward to the still waiting fiacre. Despite the bloody deed she had done, it was observed that there was not a spot of blood on her light summer dress. The soldiers cleared a way for her through the howling mob.

She was hurried into the fiacre and the two deputies got in with her. The mob closed around the vehicle, shouting for her to be delivered to them for instant vengeance. The driver was unable to move.

The danger of being lynched was now very great. This was something she had not bargained for, and she had her first moment of real weakness. She fell back on the seat half fainting. Did she imagine the crowd would hail her as a heroine and their deliverer? She was sadly misinformed about things if she did.

Drouet was a courageous and commanding man. It was he who arrested Louis XVI at Varennes. He stood up in the carriage and demanded in the name of the law and of the people that they should pass. The crowd fell back and the fiacre went on its way to the Abbaye Prison.

Charlotte Corday let out a great sigh. " Is it possible," she murmured, " that I am still alive?"

For the second time the authorities of Paris, whom she had so despised and set at naught, had saved her from a death more horrible than that of the guillotine.

And so she was taken to the Abbaye prison, safe from the vengeance of the mob.

It was two o'clock in the morning of the 14th July, 1793—the fourth anniversary of the Fall of the Bastille.

A few hours later dawn came over the tortured streets of Paris and another sweltering, feverish day began.

Both deputies and Press excitedly and passionately denounced the conspiracy which had resulted in the murder of the Friend of the People. Marat dead was now a demi-god. Robespierre and others like him were secretly pleased, for Marat stood in the way of their malevolent ambitions. Charlotte Corday had done them a good turn, but, of course, they were loud in their denunciation of her. Feverish police activity was going on in an attempt to uncover a deep-seated plot. But, though many arrests were made, no known accomplice was ever found.

The only calm spirit in Paris that day of tumult was Charlotte Corday sitting in her little cell in tranquil meditation, mending her dress and writing a letter that was to echo down a century, and cause us, even in this disillusioned decade, to stand back a little in awe of this shining girl with her terrible calm, her deadly purpose and her delicious humour.

She was the only one smiling that day in Paris. The only one who was serene and content.

Her trial was postponed for the funeral festival of Marat.

The embalmed body was carried on a chariot through the streets of Paris in splendid pomp, followed by throngs of people.

The body lay in a purple sarcophagus, and was draped in a huge tricolour, symbolic of the dressing-gown he had worn at his death. Over the edge of the sarcophagus hung a right arm, grasping a pen.

This macabre set-piece was drawn by twelve men, with white-clad girls carrying cypress boughs walking beside it. The legendary knitting women of the guillotine followed howling for the head of Charlotte Corday. Also following were deputies and government officials and bands playing the funeral march. All day long guns boomed from the Pont Neuf.

Throughout the blazing hot day the funeral revelry continued and after dark torches were lit. There was a touch of macabre comedy to the whole business when the body was brought to the place of burial under the blazing torches in the Garden of the Cordeliers. Someone seized the dangling hand to kiss it, and the arm came off. It was not Marat's arm, but merely a grim stage effect.

Charlotte Corday heard the guns and the tumult in the streets as she sat in her cell writing her immortal letter.

I have hated only one person in my life and I have proved the strength of my hatred . . . I was expecting to die at any moment, but brave men who are really above all praise, saved me from the excusable fury of those whom I had made miserable. As I really acted in cold blood, the crying of some women upset me. But if one saves one's country, one must not think of the price that has to be paid.

The monumental egotism of that last sentence is balanced by her lighthearted, almost gay attitude towards her trial.

Tomorrow at eight o'clock my trial begins. Probably by mid-day I shall have lived, to use a Latin expression. I have to have a counsel for the defence. It is the rule. I have chosen mine from the Mountain—Gustave Doulcet. I expect he will decline the honour. I thought of asking for Robespierre or Chabot!

With her philosophical resignation to her fate, nothing could touch her now, and so she was able completely to dominate the Revolutionary Tribunal at her trial.

The previous night she had secretly been transferred to a cell in the Palais de Justice near the Tribunal Chamber. This was the death cell and its furniture consisted merely of a bench clamped to the wall. Here she slept her last sleep, while outside the sultry night echoed to the uproar of her victim's bizarre funeral rights.

The Tribunal merely met to condemn her. There was no defence. There could be only one sentence.

The President was a former magistrate, Montané, and there was a jury of fourteen.

The day was even hotter and when the trial began at eight o'clock, the thermometer was already into the nineties.

The sweating crowds stared hushed at the girl standing in the dock in her light summer dress, calm and unafraid. They were totally surprised at her appearance. They expected someone quite different. Many sections of the Press had described her as a gross, coarse virago.

And so the drama began.

Gustave Doulcet, the counsel she had nominated, and whom she knew, was not there to defend her; and the President appointed Claude François Chauveau-Lagarde, a young lawyer, to represent her. Chauveau-Lagarde had the wit to see that she wished no defence, and he had to be careful, too, if he wanted to keep his own head on his shoulders.

Fouquier-Tinville, the Public Prosecutor, tried to shake her calm and humiliate her.

"How many children have you?" he demanded.

She flushed hotly. "You know I have never been married."

She identified the knife, and then Fouquier-Tinville went into detail about the skilful manner in which the blow was struck. He asked a question to which there was not an answer and which we still ask today.

She killed Marat with one blow, struck from above, which went straight into the heart with unerring aim. A person who had no previous experience of this sort of thing would find it very difficult to kill in this manner with one efficient blow.

Fouquier-Tinville's question therefore was a fair one: "Have you had previous experience?"

Her reply caused a sensation: "This monster takes me for a murderess."

It was a sublime evasion and the question still stands. Perhaps the answer is that it was a lucky blow.

The President tried hard to ring from her some admission that she had accomplices, but in vain. To some it seemed that Montané himself was being affected by the looks and beauty of the prisoner and the charm of her voice, and for these suspicions Montané later paid dearly with long years in the Bastille.

He sent a note to her counsel suggesting an insanity plea, but Chauveau-Lagarde understood his client better than that and knew the scorn with which she would reject making such a plea.

He merely said on her behalf : " Her imperturbable calm and self-abnegation which shows no sign of remorse in the very presence of death can be explained only on the basis of the political fanaticism which put the dagger into her hand. My client commends herself to the prudence of the jury."

The jury pronounced her guilty and she had nothing to say at the inevitable sentence of death. She merely turned to Chauveau-Lagarde and thanked him for defending her " in a manner worthy of yourself and me ".

It was just after mid-day of the 17th July and the execution was to take place at five o'clock that same afternoon.

She spent the few hours remaining to her posing for her portrait in the death cell and writing a letter. She refused to see a priest. The artist, Hauer, was nearly overcome with emotion. Her beauty, her dignity, her utter calmness overwhelmed him.

Her letter was to Doulcet de Pontécoulant, the counsel who failed to come to defend her.

Charlotte Corday now stood on the threshold of eternity, but this strange unbending girl had not the charity to forgive him. She wrote : " Citizen Doulcet de Pontécoulant is a coward for refusing to defend me when the task was so easy. The man who undertook it carried it out with the utmost possible dignity. I shall be grateful to him for it till my last moment—Marie de Corday."

Doulcet himself was overcome when he read this. Her previous letter had not been delivered to him, and he knew nothing about her trial until it was over. He was a brave man and would have rushed to defend her. For the rest of his life this caused him endless grief.

Sanson, the executioner, arrived in good time for her. She had another moment of weakness at the sight of him.

" What—so soon?"

Outside the crowds were gathering in the streets to cheer her on to her death. The sun had gone in at last. It was hot and humid and an angry sky was gathering over Paris.

Recovering herself quickly, Charlotte Corday submitted to the last rites—the cutting of her lovely hair.

She was ready with one of her memorable gestures. She gave Hauer a lock of her hair, which was all that she had now to offer in gratitude. He fell at her feet, weeping.

They gave her to put on the red gown worn by assassins. " My toilet of death," she called it, " which leads to immortality."

She was late for her appointment with the guillotine, and the crowds were roaring impatiently in the streets as she mounted the tumbril in the courtyard.

And as she went on her way through Paris the thunderstorm broke. It was a perfect finish, and if there had not been so many witnesses of it, one might have written the storm off as a stage effect created by the imaginations of the Corday-philes.

She stood there erect in the tumbril, hands bound behind her back, lit by flashes of lightning, the rain pouring down on her. She was soaked to the skin, but she did not flinch. The thin red smock clung wetly to her body, outlining every contour of it like the draperies of a statue.

She created an enormous impression. Some of the crowd started to cheer her. A young man threw a rose at her. Danton, Robespierre and Desmoulins watched uneasily from a window.

This was a ride of triumph. Even the heavens were saluting her courage. This courage was no myth either. Members of the Tribunal commented on it. One said that he was sorry to see condemned criminals going to the scaffold with such firmness as Charlotte Corday, and that if he were Public Prosecutor, he would have prisoners bled before execution to weaken their courage. Others commented on " this extraordinary woman who had aroused far too much interest ".

They took her the long way round, and not once did she flinch during that prolonged and terrible ride. It was nearly eight o'clock before the Place de la Révolution came in sight. The storm had now passed over and the guillotine stood out black against the forbidding sky.

36

She mounted the steps of the scaffold with a light tread, and only flinched when an assistant executioner pulled off her fichu, fearing an outrage on her modesty more than she feared the guillotine.

She wanted to speak to the people, but she was not allowed to. They seized her, tied her on the plank. The plank went forward. The knife fell and it was over.

No tumultuous roar of approval greeted the death of Charlotte Corday. She was brave and she was beautiful, and these were all human beings.

Or most of them. A moron, who had been working as an assistant at the guillotine, seized Charlotte Corday's head by the hair, held it aloft for the crowd to see and struck it on the face. The crowd did not like that, and Sanson angrily rebuked the man, who later went to prison for his deed.

There were some who said that when her head was held aloft her face was still smiling, and that it blushed at the blows.

If Charlotte Corday could have dreamed what they would do to her after her death, would she have died so unflinchingly?

The question of her character worried Revolutionary Paris. Some said she was debauched and had been the mistress of priests, royalists and Girondins. There was one way of establishing the truth.

They took her body to the Hôpital de la Charité, and there it was examined in the presence of doctors, deputies, journalists and others interested—and who wasn't?

Someone who was present did a picture of it—the body lying on a plank, the head laid to the neck, her light summer dress soaked to the waist in her blood, in the act of being removed.

What would she have thought of this final sacrilege of modesty —the ultimate outrage by which they discovered that she was without question a virgin?

After they had finished with her, they buried her in the cemetery of the Madeleine next to the remains of Louis XVI. In 1815 her bones were removed to a burial ground in the Plaine de Mousseaux, now the Plaine Monceau.

Lamartine asserted with good reason that Charlotte Corday was a pagan—a suggestion which horrified her pious nineteenth century worshippers. Was she not convent-trained, pure and chaste? The very sister of the religious Joan of Arc?

But Lamartine understood her well. In her writings her references to God were merely a courtesy. She talked not of heaven, but of Elysian fields. She had no Christian forgiveness for the unfortunate Doulcet. She read Plutarch, not the Bible. At the end she refused the consolation of a priest. Her spartan chastity had nothing to do with Christianity. She thought of herself rather as an avenging vestal virgin.

And so we come back to the vexed question of her virginity, which is perhaps the key to everything. Because she was a virgin the Victorian ladies forgave her everything. Michelet thought that, like Joan of Arc, she suffered from a prolongation of childhood.

But Théodore de Banville, writing about her in 1850, put his finger unerringly on the truth when he said:

" If she had been a wife and mother, the fair young blood that surged through her brain and heart and made her mad with fanaticism would have filled her breasts with milk to nourish beautiful children. The outrageous part of her glory and her shame was the virginity which our barbarous laws make a duty."

Gay Gibson

(1947)

CHARLOTTE CORDAY's shining virginity made her the saint among the murderesses of history—the Angel Assassin, as Lamartine called her. If she had had a lover, the romantics of her time would probably have viewed her sordid and rather stupid act of murder more in its true perspective. Limitless leniency is indeed granted to attractive young virgins.

Until recently a woman guilty of sexual immorality was at some disadvantage when up against English justice.

The immorality of both Edith Thompson (1923) and Charlotte Bryant (1936) (q.v.) no doubt counted heavily against them. Neither escaped the hangman. Nor did Margaret Allen (1949) or Ruth Ellis (1955). They were both murderesses, the former a lesbian, the latter promiscuous.

Even the twentieth century legal mind can think an immoral woman capable of anything. The first Lord Birkenhead, in attempting to justify Edith Thompson's execution, wrote: " Anyhow, she had the will to destroy her husband for the sake of her lover." This despite the fact that he confesses to a lingering doubt as to whether she was present at the crime for which she was hanged.

Gay Gibson was the reverse of the coin. She was a girl who had had various love affairs and who met her death in Cabin 126 of the *Durban Castle* on the night of 17–18 October 1947, while in the arms of a steward, James Camb.

Camb said she died while in the act of sexual intercourse

39

with him. He panicked and pushed her body out of the port-hole.

Having admitted as much to the police when the ship docked at Southampton, he was, of course, charged with her murder. Even though Camb's story might be considered to have the ring of truth about it, it is not really surprising that a British jury rejected it. What he did was callous and unforgivable. And the question that always nags in the mind in this case is that, despite his protestations to the contrary, Gay Gibson might not have been beyond medical aid when he thrust her through the port-hole into the sea.

The defence attacked Gay's morals in order to suggest that she readily accepted the steward's sexual advances, and they tried to make out that she was promiscuous. This was to combat the prosecution's theory that Camb forced his attentions on her and strangled her during the subsequent struggle.

But everyone who has travelled on liners, particularly in the tropics, knows how sexual inhibitions slacken. Any young and personable steward soon discovers how easy it is to gain access to the cabins of normally quite respectable females on these ships. Stewarding on liners is a popular job. Free sex is considered one of the perks.

For Camb's account of the death of Gay Gibson to be more or less true, she does not have to be promiscuous. Nor does he necessarily have to be a black-hearted scoundrel, even though his action in throwing the unfortunate girl's body into the sea in a moment of awful panic in the middle of the night seems un-speakably callous in the cold morning light of reason.

At Winchester Assizes the wretched Camb cut a despicable figure, and his coolness under a devastating cross-examination didn't serve him well with an English jury, suffering from post-war austerity. Talk of sex in the tropics and girls' bodies being thrown into shark-infested waters didn't strike the slightest chord of sympathy for him in their minds.

Camb in fact hadn't a chance. Perhaps he didn't deserve it. Maybe he was unlucky in picking on a girl with Gay Gibson's medical history.

But he was certainly lucky in one important respect. Parliament at the time was discussing capital punishment, and he received an automatic reprieve. He might well have been executed and taken his place among those disturbing cases in which there is a doubt, and which have served as the strongest possible argument against capital punishment.

Camb after serving about ten years in prison has now been released and has, of course, written his story for a popular Sunday newspaper.

Both counsel for the defence and prosecution have also written about Gay Gibson since the trial, and they still believe that her sexual morality is the key to the case.

Eileen Isabella Ronnie Gibson was born in India in 1926. Her parents lived in the East and sent her home to England to school. During the war she joined the Women's Auxiliary Territorial Service (the A.T.S.). She had always had stage ambitions and got herself transferred to " Stars in Battledress ". She had considerable stage talent and did well, adopting the professional name Gay Gibson.

Touring with a company of theatrical service personnel was a fairly exacting life in the days towards the end and just after the war, and she appears to have made a name for herself.

On her discharge from the services she was given the highest medical grading, but classed " non-tropical " owing to an infection of an ear. Her physical state is an important part of her tragic story.

In 1947 she travelled to South Africa with her mother to join her father, who was working at Durban. From Durban, Gay went to Johannesburg where she got a job with a local repertory company in a play called *The Silver Cord*. She was quite a success, and after several radio parts with the South African Broadcasting Company, she was offered the lead in Clifford Odet's play, *Golden Boy*, by actor-producer Henry Gilbert.

The play opened in Johannesburg in September and Gay's part required her to meet a violent death every night in company with Eric Boon, the ex-boxing champion, who had been flown out specially from England to play opposite her as the " golden boy ", the boxer with the musical longings. Although the play was well received by the Press, it closed after eleven nights, fol-

41

lowing trouble with the Johannesburg authorities over the theatre's fire precautions.

Henry Gilbert planned to take the play to Pretoria, but Gay suddenly walked out of the show, and said she was getting the next boat home.

There was little doubt that Gay was an unstable, temperamental girl. She let the rest of the cast down when there was every prospect of the play having a reasonable run, with the result that the show was unable to continue and they were all thrown out of work. Later members of the cast gave evidence at the trial, and it was said that their comments on her morals were coloured by the bitterness they felt towards her for letting them down.

There was evidence that she was not a truthful girl and was given to romancing. Eric Boon, for instance, said that she told him she left *Golden Boy* to accept an offer to play at the Gate Theatre in London. But the Gate Theatre had been closed for several years. She gave him an address in Netherall Gardens, Hampstead. But when inquiries were made later, no one there knew anything about her.

She told Mike Abel, another member of the cast of *Golden Boy*, a tissue of lies about herself—that her parents had been killed by a V2 rocket and her brothers killed in action in the Navy.

She spoke of her love affairs, including one with an elderly businessman who had paid her first-class passage in the *Durban Castle*, and also had given her £350 to spend. She told Henry Gilbert's wife, Dr. Ina Schoub, that she had had sexual experience, and that she thought she was pregnant. She also said she suffered from asthma.

Her health is of particular importance, and Dr. Schoub, a fully qualified doctor practising in Johannesburg, noticed Gay's short breath and fainting fits, and had advised her not to overstrain herself.

Mike Abel said he had seen her faint, and white saliva appeared at the corners of her mouth. Camb said he noticed bubbles at her lips when she was dying.

This is something which cannot be shrugged off as a coincidence, for Camb was not to know what Abel would say in court.

Abel also noticed the blueness of her lips and said she had complained of a pain on the underside of her left arm, which is one of the symptoms of heart trouble. Fellow members of " Stars in Battledress " had also noticed similar symptoms.

Gay was discharged from the A.T.S. with a clean bill of health, but everyone who has served in the Forces knows that medical examinations are sometimes very perfunctory. And, as asthma sufferers know, there are times when they have no trace of the complaint at all and even a doctor can't diagnose it.

Asthma comes and goes for the strangest reasons. Excitement, emotion and smells can readily bring it on. It is certainly possible that great excitement during the sexual act could produce an acute attack.

Courts of law will, of course, take notice of expert medical opinion. But, as asthma sufferers know to their cost, the medical profession can't do much for them, and indeed knows surprisingly little about asthma.

And so Gay Gibson sailed first-class in the *Durban Castle* from Capetown on 10th October 1947, in cabin No. 126—an obviously unhappy, unstable girl, discontented and probably disillusioned with life, disturbed by the war, perhaps not knowing what she wanted in the none-too-attractive world which was evolving from the devastation of 1939–45.

Those who remember those days well, and were in the services during that unreal half-world of 1939–45, know that human relationships were one of the biggest problems of life, and have nothing but admiration for the girls of that era and the way they adjusted themselves to the unnatural life which the services forced them to live. If a girl failed to adjust herself, it was probably no fault of hers.

It is easy enough to criticise the Gay Gibson which the defence presented to the Winchester Assizes in March the following year. It is easier still to picture her as the virtuous girl who was strangled while fighting an attempted rape and then thrust out of the porthole into the sea. This was the gallant but improbable theory of the prosecution which presumably was accepted by the jury, and the Court of Appeal.

The Gay Gibson who sailed from Capetown on Friday, 10th October, was bored and disappointed with life, and probably a bit desperate for companions of her own age. The *Durban Castle* was practically empty—there was no rush to get to the austerity-bound England of 1947—and most of the passengers were elderly and middle-aged.

It is no wonder that she became friendly with the agreeable young steward who was obviously strongly attracted to her. The fact that he was not admitted to her cabin until the ship was eight days out of Capetown, and half the voyage over, does not support the theory that Gay was promiscuous.

Everything suggests that he was pursuing her and that he did not find her an easy conquest.

The essence of his defence against the murder charge was that he did not need to rape her and she was only too eager to have sexual relations with him. This would be more believable if the incidents in the cabin which led to her death had taken place on the second or third day out of Capetown. But they took place eight days out. In his evidence, Camb said he met her on the second day out, and she was to all accounts about the only attractive female on the ship. It is difficult to believe that this self-confessed nautical Lothario wasn't trying hard to make her the whole time. He may have succeeded on the eighth day, when this bored, temperamental and unhappy girl finally gave in to him.

This doesn't make Gay Gibson any more immoral or promiscuous than most other females who travel on liners in these days when virginity is no longer considered anything more than a negative possession.

Let us look at the course of events as related by the various witnesses, including Camb himself, at the trial. Only Camb had reason to lie, and his evidence as to what transpired in the cabin at the time of Gay's death, though open to question, is the only account we have, and is well worth considering as a probable story.

Camb said he first fell into conversation with Gay on the

44

second day of the voyage, when she was in the Long Gallery. He said that she told him about the play she was in at Johannesburg, and that she had met a man there who had put her in the family way, but she couldn't marry him because he already had a wife. Following this improbable conversation, she asked him if he would bring tea to her cabin.

Camb was a deck steward and not allowed to go to passengers' cabins. He said they came to some compromise in which he would lay out tea trays which the bedroom steward or the night watchman would take to her cabin.

This conversation was on Sunday, the 12th. Between then and the following Friday the friendship between the attractive young passenger and the handsome young steward blossomed.

No whirlwind shipboard romance this, you will note. And it is not to be supposed that it was from want of trying that five romantic tropic nights had passed before Camb finally gained access to the lady's cabin, and she succumbed, presumably, to his fatal charm. And yet Camb's defence counsel still maintains that she practically fell over herself to get him into her bed.* It doesn't make sense.

On the evening of that tragic Friday, Gay dined with a Mr. Hopwood and Wing-Commander Bray, her usual table companions. Afterwards there was a ship's dance, a dull affair apparently, though Gay had plenty of partners.

Later there was talk of a swim in the ship's pool. It was a lovely tropic night and the *Durban Castle* was steaming past the coast of West Africa, which was about a hundred miles away on the starboard side.

At about eleven o'clock Gay went to change into her swimsuit. But she did not return for half an hour, during which time she was seen talking to Camb in the Long Gallery by James Murray, the senior nightwatchman, who overheard Camb say to her:

" I say, I have a bone to pick with you—and a big one at that."

Murray remembered this particularly, because it was a very familiar way for a steward to talk to a passenger.

Camb said this referred to the tea-tray he had set out for her

---

* *A Lance For Liberty*, by J. D. Casswell, Q.C. (Harrap, 1961)

earlier, and which she had not bothered to collect. He was angry about it, but it was nothing more than the anger of a man who felt possessive about a girl whom he ardently desired, and whose favours he had not so far found easy to win.

Gay was contrite about the untouched tea-tray and asked him to leave her a rum for later that night. She was so friendly, in fact, said Camb, that he determined there and then to push his advantage.

Gay went to her cabin for her swimsuit, and he followed her there. Perhaps she would like a supper tray as well? he suggested. Or some lemonade with the rum?

She told him she wanted neither supper tray nor lemonade with her rum, and he found her manner sufficiently provocative to say to her:

" I've half a mind to bring a drink down and join you."

" Please yourself," she replied lightly.

This was the green light for Camb, who found her attitude tantalisingly encouraging. Unable to find her swimsuit, Gay left the cabin, telling him to leave the rum in the usual place.

It was about eleven-thirty when Gay returned to her fellow passengers, and about a half an hour later Hopwood escorted her to her cabin. He opened the door, turned on the lights for her, said good night, and retired to his own cabin.

At one o'clock the boatswain's mate was in charge of a working party swabbing down the deck when he saw the lonely figure of a girl leaning on the rail at the after end of the Promenade Deck, cigarette smoke curling around her head in the warm tropic night. He went up to her.

" Are you all right, miss?"

Gay Gibson turned. Her black evening dress clung to her slim body.

" Yes, thank you. I came up for a breath of air. It's rather warm below."

The mate told her they were swabbing the Promenade Deck, and directed her to a part of the deck where she would not get wet.

She murmured her thanks and walked away, the mate watching her, noticing her silver dancing shoes. Then he turned to his work, not dreaming that the girl was walking to her death. He was the last person to see her alive—apart from the man who was found guilty of her murder.

The story is now his to tell. After ten years in prison he tells the same story. If he told a different one, the law could not touch him, for he has been punished for Gay Gibson's murder, whether he admits to the murder or not.

Camb was stacking away chairs while Gay was alone on deck, smoking, gazing out to sea and thinking—thinking about what?

About one o'clock he came across her on deck, the glass of rum in her hand, smoking a cigarette. After exchanging a few words with her, he returned to his work. It was not advisable to be seen dallying with a female passenger at that time of night. Camb's explanation for his subsequent behaviour is that it was motivated by his fear of losing his job, as he would have done if found in a passenger's cabin for sexual purposes.

Just after one o'clock he locked the pantry and went to Cabin 126. The light was on. He knocked and went in, but Gay was not there. He went forward to the crew well deck and waited for about an hour. A little after two he returned to the cabin and found her there.

She was in a yellow quilted dressing-gown which had a zip right down the front. She was lying on the bed drinking her rum. He sat on the edge of the bed and they chatted for about a quarter of an hour, their conversation embracing such things as the dullness of the ship's dance that night.

Gay finished her rum and put the empty glass on the dressing-table beside her. Camb, who was wearing only a sleeveless vest and trousers, got on the bed with her and took her in his arms.

She raised no objection, and in fact, according to him, she unzipped her dressing-gown, underneath which she was invitingly naked.

After some preliminary sex play, copulation took place, with him lying in the more usual position on top of her. Her head was in the crook of his left arm, and his right hand was resting

47

on her hip. Her right arm was around his neck and her left hand was holding his right arm.

Gay Gibson died just as, in Camb's own words in court, "intercourse would normally have come to an end." When a man uses a phrase like this he usually means the point at which he reaches his climax. A skilful lover, however, terminates the act only when his partner has had satisfaction also.

It is impossible to pursue this point, of course, though it might well have some bearing on Gay's death, if she did, as Camb maintains, die suddenly during the act of intercourse without any violence on his part.

According to him, at the moment of climax, "she suddenly heaved under me as though she was gasping for breath—as though she was taking a deep breath. Her body stiffened for a fraction of a second, and then relaxed completely limp. Her right arm was still round my neck when she heaved against me. That arm automatically tightened and the left arm holding my right forearm, gripped tightly. All this happened in a matter of seconds."

"I immediately got off the bed," continued Camb in court. "She was completely relaxed as though she was in a dead faint. One eye was just slightly open. Her mouth was open a little, too. There was a faint line of bubbles, which I assumed to be froth, just on the edges of her lips. It was a muddy colour, and appeared to be slightly blood-flecked.

"First of all I listened and felt for her heart-beats. I could not find any, and I attempted, by massaging the stomach towards the heart to bring back circulation."

Camb's description of Gay Gibson's death was accepted by the pathologist, Professor J. M. Webster, as being so consistent with the result of a heart attack that he was prepared to give evidence for Camb at his trial.

Gay's previous medical history, too, was such that she might well have died in this sudden and unexpected way in a moment of considerable physical excitement. It is certainly not unusual for a woman to faint during a sexual orgasm. Is not death just that one stage further?

It is perhaps worth emphasising at this point that during his

48

Charlotte Corday

Assassination
of Marat

trial Camb had no idea of what Professor Webster, or indeed any other witness for the defence, would say in the box. We have Mr. J. D. Casswell's assurance on this point, and the assurance of a Queen's Counsel of such distinction and eminence is good enough for anyone.

Mr. Casswell, writing years later about this case, is still puzzled why the jury were not impressed by Professor Webster's most telling evidence.

The professor said that he knew of at least three cases in which death suddenly occurred naturally during the act of intercourse, without any violence by the other party. In each of these cases the person who died was healthy, and showed no signs of a health defect which might have caused such a thing to happen. One was a 28-year-old man who was in the Army at the time.

Professor Webster thought that death during the sexual act could be attributed to one of two causes. Firstly, the bursting of a small congenital aneurism in the brain, a condition which could not be diagnosed during life. Secondly, heart disease.

In a girl of Gay Gibson's age the most likely cause would be indirect heart disease, caused either by a septic focus somewhere else in the body, such as a chronic running ear, or through the effect of asthma on her heart.

We know that she suffered from both of these conditions. Her ear trouble was noted in her medical discharge papers, and there is plenty of evidence that she had asthma.

Professor Webster's opinion was backed up by another pathologist, Dr. Hocking.

But even if the jury were not convinced by the medical opinion that there was a reasonable chance that Gay Gibson's death might have been caused through the state of her health, the lingering doubt remains, and Camb's story of what happened in Cabin 126 that night is worth pursuing.

It was between two and three o'clock in the morning of Saturday the 18th that this desperate drama was taking place in Gay Gibson's cabin. The *Durban Castle* drove northwards into the sultry tropic night. Everything was normal to the officer on the watch. From the bridge he heard no splash over the side,

D

and, if he had, it might have been a flying fish, a porpoise, or even a shark.

Except for the night watch, nearly everyone in the ship was asleep. Only Gay Gibson would not see the new day which would soon dawn over the distant African shore.

In the galley on A Deck, Murray, the senior nightwatchman, and his assistant Steer, were on duty.

At 2.58 they heard a buzzing over their heads which indicated that someone was ringing from a cabin on an upper deck. The bell-push in any cabin set a glowing trail of lights leading to the cabin from which the call had come.

Steer followed the trail of lights. It led him to Cabin 126. Two more lights, one red and one green, were showing outside the door, which told him that the occupant had rung for both steward and stewardess. This was unusual, for a passenger would normally ring for either one or the other.

Steer could see the cabin light shining through the fanlight over the door. He knocked, then opened the door, which was not bolted.

He only managed to push the door open a little way, for someone was on the other side. He glimpsed the face of Camb, who said, " All right," and then slammed the door in Steer's face.

Steer returned to the galley on A Deck and told Murray what had happened. The two of them then went to Gay Gibson's cabin, and stood outside the door for about ten minutes, trying to make up their minds what to do.

Murray had previously heard Camb talking to Gay in a familiar fashion, so he could not have been surprised that he was in her cabin at three o'clock in the morning. It was not an un-usual happening. What puzzled Murray was the fact that both bell-pushes had been pressed.

What was going on in there?

Not a sound came from the cabin inside which poor Gay Gibson's last drama was being played out in grim silence as Camb worked desperately to get himself out of an appalling situation.

He said he tried artificial respiration, but could get no spark of life back into Gay's limp body. He desperately searched for smelling salts, but could find none.

Who rang the bells?

The defence theory was that Camb's hip accidentally touched the bell buttons while he was trying to revive Gay. This was demonstrably possible.

The prosecution maintained that the ringing of the night bells was the last desperate act of Gay as she was being assaulted and strangled.

In that case, as one must assume that Camb had been in her cabin nearly an hour before she summoned help, it is much to the point to ask what was happening during that hour. Was she resisting him? Arguing with him? Struggling with him?

Mrs. Henrietta Stephens, who was in the next cabin, lying within a few inches of Gay Gibson's bed, said she heard no suspicious sounds.

Camb's later attitude suggested that he had no idea how the bells had been pushed.

And why, if Camb's intention was to assault and rape, did he not lock the cabin door? This unlocked door is surely of considerable significance.

Meanwhile, Steer and Murray went up to the bridge and reported to the officer of the watch what had happened. But they did not want to get Camb into trouble, so they suggested that the man they had seen was another passenger. The officer of the watch proposed to do nothing about it. The passengers' morals were not his concern.

But supposing Murray had strictly done his duty and told the officer of the watch that a steward was in the cabin of a passenger who was ringing for help? Obviously an entry would have been quickly forced into Cabin 126, perhaps in time to save Gay going through the porthole. In which case the outcome of the story might have been a very different one.

Steer and Murray were not to know. They went back on duty. But Murray wasn't satisfied. He knew something odd was happening in Cabin 126. He returned there to find the cabin lights out, and all was silence. He did not attempt to go in.

While all these hushed and whispered comings and goings were taking place outside in the alleyway, Camb, according to his story, was wrestling with the appalling problem of what to do.

He was certain that Gay Gibson was dead. Her body was getting cold. He was panic-stricken. He knew that being discovered in a lady's cabin meant instant dismissal, with no chance of getting a job with any other shipping line.

It was an incredibly selfish way of viewing the problem. And could he really be so sure that she was dead—beyond all hope of resuscitation by expert medical aid?

" I confess now," he said later, " that it sounds very foolish, but I hoped to give the impression that she had fallen overboard and deny all knowledge of having been in the cabin in the hope that the Captain's further inquiries might not be too severe."

His only concern was to get rid of the body. It did not occur to him to summon medical aid for Gay. Nor did he seem to think that the best way of substantiating his story of how she died—and he was surely intelligent enough to think that he *might* be called upon to substantiate it—was for her body to be examined medically. If his story was true, he would lose his job, but he wouldn't be charged with murder.

Instead he panicked and tried to get rid of the body—easy to do as Gay was slim enough to go through the porthole.

He thus exposed himself to the unanswerable accusation that he believed that, with no body, he could not be charged with murder. This belief is quite false, though widely held.

From this, the question follows: If he had not committed murder, why the desperate necessity to dispose of Gay's body? Did he place such a high price on his precious job as a ship's steward?

One can believe that he did not care twopence about the wretched Gay. She was just another sexual episode for him, and he had had what he wanted from her. His first concern when facing the police at Southampton was that his wife should not know what he got up to with the women passengers when he was at sea.

52

One can believe, too, in his panic—with the two watchmen prowling suspiciously outside the door. He did not believe that Steer had recognised him, and he thought he was going to get away with it. But he knew a report would immediately be made to the officer of the watch.

He panicked, he said, because he didn't want to lose his job.

So he lifted Gay Gibson as she was in her yellow-quilted dressing-gown and pushed her head first through the porthole into the sea.

Later he had to admit in a devastating cross-examination at Winchester Assizes that, merely in order to avoid losing his job, he had deliberately failed to call for help, although this might, so far as he could tell, have saved Gay Gibson's life. He had also destroyed the evidence of his innocence. If he had strangled her, the marks of his hands would have been found around her neck. If she had died in the way he asserted she did, that too could have been established by a pathologist.

Even his own counsel admitted that his action was selfish, brutal and cruel, and Camb freely admitted in court that he was ashamed of himself, and that it was beastly conduct to save himself by failing to call medical attention for the stricken Gay Gibson.

At his trial Camb had to face another awkward question. What had happened to Gay's black pyjamas?

The stewardess said that at 7.30 on the morning of the 18th, she went into Cabin 126, found it empty, and began to tidy it, thinking Gay Gibson was in the bathroom. Both her pyjamas and dressing-gown were missing.

What had happened to them?

The prosecution insisted that she must have been wearing them all the time and was not in the state of inviting nudity which Camb described. If she had willingly had sexual intercourse with him it was reasonable to suppose that she would have taken them off.

Camb was unable to answer this. He did not know what had happened to the pyjamas. His counsel, when he saw him in Winchester prison, pressed him on the point, telling him that if he had got rid of the pyjamas he might as well say so. But he insisted he knew nothing of the pyjamas, both privately to his counsel, and also under pressure in court from judge as well as counsel. In the same way, he knew nothing of how the bells came to be rung.

Gay had certainly lost her swimsuit. Was it possible that she had lost her pyjamas too?

Although Camb was found guilty, his story of the way Gay Gibson died has the ring of truth about it, and he stuck to it throughout the rigours of a gruelling cross-examination. And to this day he sticks to it.

It must be admitted that it fits into such facts as are known about Gay Gibson's health. It must be admitted too, that, given the man's character, it is the sort of thing he would be expected to do.

The two counsel who fought the case at Winchester Assizes, years later published their considered views about it.

Camb's counsel, Mr. J. D. Casswell, Q.C., firmly believes his client's story, and quotes Mr. Justice Humphreys as saying after the appeal: "That young man wasn't given a chance." Mr. Casswell thinks that Camb had only his own folly and callousness to blame for the guilty verdict.

"Luckily—and I used this word advisedly when dealing with a case where even today [1961] there is still so much room for doubt—Camb was not executed."

Mr. G. D. Roberts, Q.C., who prosecuted, holds the forthright opinion that Camb "is the luckiest killer alive".

He just does not accept Camb's story and states something which could not be brought out at the trial—" that Camb was known to have assaulted women passengers on three different occasions in the *Durban Castle* . . . he nearly strangled a woman in a shelter on the deck."*

It could not, of course, have altered the verdict if such allegations could have been made at the trial. Camb was found guilty and that was that. Mr. Roberts is merely trying to assure us that the verdict was just.

This raises the point which both the A6 murder and the Hume

---

* An article in *Titbits*, 19th January 1963.

case have emphasised. Is the English system of justice so superior after all?

In continental countries the courts are as much concerned about the background and personal history of the accused as they are about the crime he is accused of. The continental courts probe deeper than do the English, which are straitjacketed by strict rules and conventions. Many people now think that true justice is more likely to be arrived at under the continental system.

This strong criticism of English justice has been growing in recent years and the public are slowly coming to realise that our legal system is by no means the perfect instrument which we have always been led to believe. The fact that an English court, in all its majesty, can become an object of comedy so much more readily than a continental court can is surely a reason for unease.

It is certainly as important for the court to know the kind of person they are trying, as to know the circumstances of the particular crime of which he is accused. But this vital information, generally speaking, is denied to an English jury.

In Camb's case, the allegations now made by Mr. G. D. Roberts would in a practical common-sense system of justice have been put before the Winchester Assizes at the trial and proved or disproved. Camb's character and history were just as important as his actions.

English legal minds will probably defend the existing system to the last ditch and strongly resent lay criticism of their sacred citadel. But perhaps legal minds are not the best ones to judge their own well entrenched theories and practices. The legal mind is notoriously behind the times. In the last century it stoutly defended hanging children for stealing. In this century some of our legal men are still in favour of flogging and hanging.

And as for Gay Gibson, she was just another of the long line of unfortunates whose personal tragedies pattern the history of crime. Whatever was the secret of her last hour, she will be remembered with pity.

For as long as crime is discussed she will not be forgotten, for her death fully established the important point that a man can be successfully charged with murder, even though no trace is found of the body of his victim.

Starr Faithfull
(1931)

THE STRANGE death of Starr Faithfull in June 1931 added not only a poetic name to the mysteries of crime, but provided an unusual and fascinating character which has intrigued writers and film makers for the past thirty-five years.

At least two novels have been written about her. One, *Butterfield 8*, by John O'Hara, was made into a film in which Elizabeth Taylor starred. But the real story of Starr Faithfull is a much more interesting one than the somewhat pallid drama which Miss Taylor enacted on the screen.

The abiding mystery of Starr's death will provide her with a certain immortality. The pitiful tragedy of her ruined life arouses familiar echoes in these days now that the sexual side of her strange story is more readily understood and can be more freely discussed.

She was the daughter of a Frank W. Wyman, and her mother came from Boston and was distantly related to Andrew J. Peters, a wealthy ex-congressman who had been Mayor of Boston.

Starr used to play with the Peters' children on the beach, and, it was stated later by her stepfather, Stanley Faithfull, she had been seduced by the middle-aged Mr. Peters when she was eleven, the child's seduction being effected by the use of ether.

This relationship with Peters continued for several years. It had, of course, a profound effect upon the girl's life. She became an ether addict, drank heavily, and consumed large quantities of barbiturates. A drug of some sort was always essential to her when she was indulging in sex.

For a while her relationship with Peters—she always referred to him as A.J.P.—was unknown to her parents, who were puzzled at the strange phases Starr went through. She would not go swimming because she thought it was indecent to wear a bathing suit. She wore ankle-length dresses at a time when the universal fashion was knee-length. She wore boys' clothes and refused to associate with any friends of her own age. She locked herself in her room for days reading philosophy and poetry.

In the early twenties, when Starr was about fifteen, her mother divorced Frank Wyman and married a retired manufacturing chemist named Stanley E. Faithfull. The name Faithfull was readily adopted by Starr and her young sister, Tucker.

The Faithfulls lived in a second-floor apartment at 12 St. Luke's Place, Greenwich Village, New York, an attractive house with an early New York façade. The apartment cost $85 a month rent and contained in it more than $15,000 worth of Chippendale, Sheraton and Empire furniture. The source of the Faithfull family income was always a mystery and the subject of much speculation.

While still in her teens Starr led an irregular sex life. Her early sex experiences robbed her of any enjoyment in the act itself, yet sex was an important part of her life. She confessed that it was the preliminaries which counted with her. In this fact may lie the key to the mystery of her death. She would spend hours tantalising a man before either she gave in to him or he forcibly took what she was tormenting him with. What dark, indelible terror in her past bred this state of mind can readily be guessed.

She kept a diary which she called her Mem Book, written in a kind of shorthand in which there were no names, only initials, and which told clearly enough of her bitterness and frustration. It contained erotic passages quite unpublishable, and had many references to A.J.P. Some of these references were full of hatred; others contained a certain affection. But in them all was a sick fear of him. " Spent night A.J.P. Providence. Oh, Horror, Horror, Horror ! ! !"

58

After she had spent two nights at a New York hotel with A.J.P. —she was still in her teens—she told her mother about him.

What Mrs. Faithfull's reaction was to the story of her distinguished kinsman's conduct is not known. But what is known is that the Faithfull family were paid a large sum of money for signing a formal release to an unnamed individual quitting him in lengthy terms of all liability for damage done to Starr.

Stanley Faithfull himself said that the sum involved was $20,000, which had all been spent on medical and psychiatric treatment for Starr. The Boston solicitors who negotiated the agreement commented: " If Mr. Faithfull wants to say it was only $20,000, then we're satisfied to let it rest at that."

But it was freely said that the Faithfull family had got $80,000 out of the intimidated Mr. Peters for the damage done to young Starr and had been living on the money for years.

As for Mr. Peters himself, he merely issued a formal denial that he had ever indulged in improper relations with Starr Faithfull and no proceedings were ever taken against him.

This then was the background for Starr Faithfull's formative years. The celebrated Lolita of thirty years later seems just a precocious innocent beside Starr with her elaborately developed perversions and masochistic sex-play.

Starr received treatment from several psycho-analysts, but, judging from what happened afterwards, it did not do her much good.

About a year before her death, people heard screams coming from a room in a New York hotel and called the police. A patrolman went into the room and found Starr lying naked on the bed. With her was an infuriated man clad only in his undershirt, who had obviously been beating her up. On the table was a half-empty bottle of gin.

The man gave his name as Joseph Collins. He didn't even know the girl's name. The policeman told him to get out, which Collins did—never to be seen or heard of again. Starr was taken to Bellevue Hospital.

Scenes of this kind are not unusual in certain hotels in big cities, and the patrolman's cynical incuriosity about the encounter is not really surprising. He probably assumed that Starr was what is known in the London underworld as a pussy-girl or a slapparat.

A pussy-girl is a prostitute who will hire herself out to a sadist to be whipped and flogged. She is not a pervert. She is in it for the money, and there is big money in it. It seems that flogging and whipping is a perversion of the rich.

A slapparat, on the other hand, is a female masochist, who will allow the most unpleasant things to be done to her for the sheer joy of suffering. She has to meet her male—or even female —counterpart, and these introductions are effected by certain members of the London and New York underworlds who specialise in catering for the sex-crazy. The sadist is called a bundler, and there is good authority for saying that the slapparats and pussy-girls of London number some very wealthy and influential people among their clients.

Whereas a pussy-girl sets a definite limit to what the bundler may do to her, the slapparat doesn't, and she sometimes gets killed during the sadistic orgy.

Such a case was that of Margery Gardner who was beaten up and killed by Neville George Heath in a hotel in Notting Hill, London, in 1945. Margery Gardner was plainly a slapparat, but Heath's next victim, Doreen Marshall, was a normal girl who had the misfortune to fall for the Heath charm. Perhaps if Heath had stuck to slapparats he might have got away with it, for there are cases when the slapparat has died and the bundler has escaped a murder charge by confessing their mutual perversion.

Starr Faithfull was not to be numbered among this rather dreary class of human being. Her aberration was a little more complicated, even if her end was just as inevitable.

There is good reason to believe that she had driven Joseph Collins to breaking point with the endless " preliminaries " which meant so much to her.

When she got to Bellevue she told the doctors : " I was drinking gin, as far as I know. This is the first time I have had anything to drink for six months. I don't know how many I had. I suppose somebody knocked me around a bit."

Her hospital record stated: "Brought to hospital by Flower Hospital ambulance. Noisy and unsteady. Acute alcoholism. Contusions face, jaw and upper lip. Given medication. Went to sleep. Next a.m. noisy, crying. People came. Discharged."

Starr made two trips to England, the first with her mother and sister, the second alone. On the first occasion she cut something of a dash at London parties during the Charleston era with her striking appearance and beautiful clothes. On her second visit to London, she tried to commit suicide. She was found in time and twenty-four grains of allonal were pumped out of her.

After this she seemed to develop a nostalgia for England—or perhaps it was just for the sea. Anyway, she had no money for a trans-Atlantic trip, but she haunted the docks in New York where the Europe-bound liners were berthed, and joined in the pre-sailing parties, leaving the ship with infinite reluctance, always at the last minute.

In the last few weeks of her life—she was now twenty-five— she met a young Englishman, George Jameson-Carr, who was a surgeon on the *Franconia*, a 20,000-ton Cunarder, popular in her day both as a cruising ship and on the Atlantic run.

She fell passionately in love with Dr. Jameson-Carr. He did not reciprocate the emotion, and was in fact quite embarrassed by her eager attentions.

On 29th May 1931, she went on board the *Franconia* shortly before it sailed for Southampton. She had already had a lot to drink.

This was during Prohibition and her stepfather, warning her against speakeasy gin, used to mix her a flask of Martinis to take with her. On this day her flask was empty and she was tight in her usual noisy, flamboyant way. She was on the *Franconia* seeking more to drink as well as pursuing the ship's surgeon.

Dr. Jameson-Carr managed to get rid of his not very welcome guest well before sailing time, but although she left his sitting-room, she did not go ashore. The *Franconia* sailed and was well down the bay before her presence was discovered among the other passengers.

The ship was stopped and she was put on a shore-going tugboat, after creating a scene which she made highly embarrassing for Jameson-Carr.

The next day, May 30th, she wrote him the following letter:

I am going (definitely now—I've been thinking of it for a long time) to end my worthless, disorderly bore of an existence—before I ruin everyone else's life as well. I certainly have made a sordid, futureless mess of it all. I am dead, dead sick of it. It is no one's fault but my own—I hate everything so—life is horrible. Being a sane person, you may not understand—I take dope to forget and drink to try and like people, but it is of no use.

I am mad and insane over you. I hold my breath to try and stand it—take allonal in the hope of waking happier, but that homesick feeling never leaves me. I have, strangely enough, more of a feeling of peace or whatever you call it now that I know it will soon be over. The half-hour before I die will, I imagine, be quite blissful.

You promised to come to see me. I realise absolutely that it will be the one and only time. There is no earthly reason why you should come. If you do it will be what I call an act of marvellous generosity and kindness. What I did yesterday was very horrible, although I don't see how you could lose your job, as it must have been clearly seen what a nuisance you thought me.

If I don't see you again—good-bye. Sorry to lose all sense of humour, but I am suffering so that all I want is to have it over with. It's become such a hell as I couldn't have imagined.

If you come to see me when you are in this time you will be a sport—you are assured by this letter of no more bother from me. My dear—

Starr.

On 2nd June, she wrote him a formal note of apology, regretting her conduct on the ship and saying that he had not invited her to come aboard or had served her with any drinks. She had brought her own liquor and had drunk it too hastily. She assured him that she would never embarrass him again, and signed it "Yours very sincerely, Starr Faithfull". This was obviously written so that he could show it to his employers, should it be necessary.

She wrote him a third letter on 4th June—the day she disappeared. It was posted at 4.30 p.m. and was written on the stationery of a department store writing-room. It said:

Hello, Bill old thing:

It's all up with me now. This is something I am going to put through. The only thing that bothers me about it—the only thing I dread—is being outwitted and prevented from doing this, which is the only possible thing for me to do. If one wants to get away with murder, one has to jolly well keep one's wits about one. It's the same way with suicide. If I don't watch out I will wake up in a psychopathic ward, but I intend to watch out and accomplish my end this time. No ether, allonal, or window jumping. I don't want to be maimed. I want oblivion. If there is an after life, it would be a dirty trick—but I am sure fifty million priests are wrong. That is one of those things one knows.

Nothing makes any difference now. I love to eat, and can have one delicious meal with no worry over gaining. I adore music and am going to hear some good music. I believe I love music more than anything. I am going to drink slowly, keeping aware every second. Also I am going to enjoy my last cigarettes. I won't worry because men flirt with me in the streets—I shall encourage them—I don't care who they are. I'm afraid I've always been a rotten " sleeper "; it's the preliminaries that count with me. It doesn't matter though.

It's a great life when one has twenty-four hours to live. I can be rude to people. I can tell them they are too fat or that I don't like their clothes, and I don't have to dread being a lonely old woman, or poverty, obscurity, or boredom. I don't have to dread living on without ever seeing you, or hearing rumours such as " the women all fall for him ", and " he entertains charmingly ". Why in hell shouldn't you? But it's more than I can cope with, this feeling I have for you. I have tried to pose as clever and intellectual, thereby to attract you, but it was not successful, and I couldn't go on writing those

63

long, studied letters. I don't have to worry because there are no words in which to describe this feeling I have for you. The words love, adore, worship have become meaningless. There is nothing I can do but what I am going to do. I shall never see you again. That is extraordinary. Although I can't comprehend the words "always"—or "time", they produce a very merciful numbness.

Starr.

I have quoted these last two letters of hers in full not only because of the illumination they throw upon the mind of this strange and unhappy girl, but because they may provide an important clue to what happened to her.

They show such a calm and determined resolve for suicide that it is only the very peculiar circumstances of her death which makes us think again.

If Starr Faithfull was so completely determined upon suicide, by what cynical stroke of fate was it that she met her death in another way? That is the fascinating mystery here. Is it believable that fate intervened in such a fashion? Did she court death by treading the path she knew so well, driven on irresistibly by those strange agonies of desire and repulsion which had their roots in that indelible experience all those years ago in Boston?

4th June was the day she disappeared from home—the day she wrote her last letter to Jameson-Carr. She was in her usual spirits—an alternating depression and gaiety. The family were broke apparently and could only spare her three dollars. Nobody asked where she was going, or when she would be back, and she did not say. It was that kind of home.

All the same Stanley Faithfull was in his own way devoted to this rather bewildering girl who had become his stepdaughter, and whom he could never understand, and when she failed to return that night he was very worried. He went to police headquarters first thing in the morning and reported her absence to the Missing Persons Bureau, and then phoned all her friends and acquaintances for news of her.

On 8th June, her body, clad in a silk dress and nothing else,

Gay Gibson

Dusting the door for fingerprints in the cabin of *Durban Castle* where Gay Gibson died

was found washed up by the tide on Long Beach by Daniel Moriarty, a beachcomber.

The first autopsy showed that she had died by drowning and that her body had been in the water for at least forty-eight hours. She had taken two grains of veronal—enough perhaps to cause unconsciousness, but not enough to cause death, but no alcohol was found in the body. She had eaten a large meal. her lungs were full of sand. There was extensive bruising of the upper part of the body, caused by human hands. She had been raped before death.

A second autopsy discounted the rape theory, but established that sexual intercourse had taken place shortly before death.

This fabulous piece of flotsam with the wonderful name made one of the best newspaper stories of the year, especially when the mystery of her death deepened and the strange story of her life was revealed.

The Faithfull home in Greenwich Village was under constant siege by reporters. The real story of Starr's life, as told by Stanley Faithfull, was secured exclusively by a Press syndication, and all that the other reporters got were unimportant details, with the result that there was a lot of uncomplimentary speculation about the Faithfull household in the New York tabloids.

It was certainly an interesting household. Morris Markey, who was the original " Reporter at Large " for the New Yorker, writes (in *The Aspirin Age*, Simon & Schuster, New York 1949) : " There were to be sure manifestations of eccentricity in great abundance in this family." He went calling on the Faithfulls one evening while the story was at its height and the house was surrounded by reporters.

Mr. Faithfull was standing thoughtfully in the doorway of his living-room, a big pipe in one hand and a volume of the *Encyclopaedia Britannica* in the other.

" Come in," he said. " I was just trying to determine the normal weight of the human liver. There are some things in that last autopsy report I don't like, and I'd like to satisfy myself. Do you know how to translate grams into pounds and ounces?"

65

Mrs. Faithfull came in—a thin woman with what we used to call the touch of good breeding upon her, wearing a nervous smile and offering hospitality in words that tumbled over each other.

" I'm quite relieved it is just you," she said. " We thought it might be the police to take Tucker away. One of the reporters told us an hour ago they were coming . . ."

" Would it be possible for me to meet Tucker?"

" Why, certainly."

(Remember that I had never been in the Faithfull home before, never met one member of the family before.)

Tucker was in bed reading a book, taking the whole thing very calmly, said Markey. She showed him a bunch of telegrams with offers from Broadway, movie scouts, night-club owners, vaudeville people and agents.

With Starr's sensational story dominating the front pages, the family received permission to cremate the body. Starr's real father, Frank Wyman, suddenly turned up and, with Mr. and Mrs. Faithfull and Tucker, attended the funeral service.

They were kneeling in front of the candle-lit bier when there was a dramatic interruption. Men from the office of the District Attorney rushed in and stopped the funeral. The D.A. had received new evidence and ordered a further post-mortem.

The following day the D.A. stated : " I know the identity of the two men who killed Starr Faithfull. One of them is a prominent New York politician. They took her to Long Beach, drugged her and held her head under the water until she was drowned. I will arrest both of them within thirty-six hours."

But no arrests were ever made. No prominent New Yorkers became involved in the scandal.

At this point the Starr Faithfull story took a new turn. Until now, no one in America knew of the suicide letters she had written to Dr. Jameson-Carr. On 23rd June, Jameson-Carr arrived in New York with them. He was described as " a pleasant fellow cast in a difficult and highly embarrassing rôle ". He hoped that the letters would clear up the whole mystery.

Stanley Faithfull said the letters were forgeries, but handwriting experts proved beyond doubt that the hand which wrote the erotic Mem Book also wrote the letters.

The murder theory seemed to be disposed of by the letters, and the case dropped out of the headlines. Interest in it quickly died.

All the same, despite the letters, the evidence pointed strongly against suicide. The bruising and the sand in the lungs suggests that she had been held forcibly head down in the shallows and drowned. In the light of the medical evidence, suicide is ruled out. If she had drowned herself by going into the sea or jumping off one of the liners, as had been suggested, there would have been no sand in her lungs.

Her coat, underclothes and shoes were never found. If she had committed suicide, they surely would have been.

The most likely explanation of her death is to be found in her curious sex life. The Joseph Collins episode may provide a valuable clue. Some such orgy may have taken place on the lonely Long Island beach. Her desire to prolong the preliminaries to the point of non-consummation may have resulted in violence.

Morris Markey thinks that she teased this unknown man beyond endurance. He became violent, mauled her, perhaps into unconsciousness, panicked, took her to the water's edge and held her head under.

Recall for a moment her last letter to Jameson-Carr when she was discussing what she was going to do during her last twenty-four hours. She talked about the " one delicious meal " she would have without worrying about putting on weight. According to the autopsy, she had certainly had that.

" I won't worry because men flirt with me in the streets—I shall encourage them—I don't care who they are." This corroborates the theory that she had allowed a stranger to pick her up.

But does it fit into her declared determination to end her life? What was she doing having a sex orgy on a Long Island beach with a strange man if she was hopelessly in love with another man and wanted to end her life because he did not return her love?

Does it make sense even on the Markey theory of the last

67

fling, the final attempt to put the panting male in his place, to torture him and ridicule his excitement—"the male who lay eternally on her mind as the male who had hurt and frightened her and savagely disillusioned her so long ago in Boston"?

Did she indeed invite, in this violent way, the death she so ardently desired?

We will never know the answer. Starr Faithfull died as she lived—an enigma.

Marguerite Diblanc

(1872)

SEVENTY-EIGHT YEARS after the famous assassinating angel descended upon Paris, another formidable young woman, also destined for her brief moment in the bright limelight accorded to killers of important people, was fighting at the barricades of the beleaguered city shoulder-to-shoulder with the comrades of the 1871 Commune.

Marguerite Diblanc was no Charlotte Corday. She was no beauty, no aristocrat. She had neither bearing nor personality. She was in fact a Belgian cook. Her crime was sordid and undistinguished. Her victim was not even famous.

It was the circumstances of the crime which distinguished it. It touched upon the lives of the great, and revealed one of those cosy Victorian sex scandals which we find so endearing in these days of complicated sexuality.

It also touched upon the glories of two inglorious wars. The Charge of the Light Brigade in 1854 and the Battle of the Barricades in Paris in 1871 were two highlights of heroism in two unnecessary wars in which tens of thousands of innocent people were slaughtered because of the obstinacy and stupidity of a few men.

We can trace the story right back to 1826 when Lord Lucan, then Lord Bingham, bought the 17th Lancers over the head of Captain Anthony Bacon, who was a friend of Edward Gibbon Wakefield, the abductor of Ellen Turner (q.v.). Bacon was a brilliant cavalry officer, and had he been in command of the British cavalry at Balaclava he would not have sent the Light Brigade to its celebrated doom as Lord Lucan did. But wealth and aristocracy were more important than intelligence and talent in nineteenth-century England, and Lucan was able to put up £25,000, so he got the 17th Lancers.

He and his brother-in-law, the Earl of Cardigan, commanded the cavalry between them during the Crimean War. *The Times* war correspondent of the day, wrote of them : " We all agree that two greater muffs than Lucan and Cardigan could not be." A fellow officer wrote : " Two such fools could hardly be picked out of the British Army. And they take command. But they are earls ! "

This was before Balaclava. The disaster of the famous charge was entirely their doing, Lucan, who was in command of the cavalry, having the greater responsibility. An official inquiry in 1856 established this as a matter of history.

Despite this, Lucan survived long enough to live it down. Twenty years later, loaded with military honours, he was living luxuriously on the proceeds of his Irish estates, from which the starving peasantry were fleeing to America as fast as immigrant ships could carry them. He was living in England. His name was cursed in Ireland, where they called him " the exterminator " owing to the ruthless oppression of his tenants during the famines of the nineteenth century.

His London address was 36 South Street, Mayfair. He had taken a French mistress, a Madame Marie Caroline Besson Riel, whom he had installed in January 1871 at 13 Park Lane. His countess lived at Laleham, the family estate in Middlesex.

In 1872, Marie Riel was forty-six and Lucan was seventy-two. She was a widow and had a daughter, Julie, who was in her twenties, an actress, who at the time was playing a series of French comedies at the St. James's Theatre.

From all accounts, Marie Riel was a bad-tempered woman with a biting tongue who gave her servants hell. But she must have had some considerable charm for the noble Earl of Lucan, who not only paid the rent of her most desirable house in Park Lane, but also gave her a handsome allowance. He could well afford the best in the way of mistresses.

Lucan's love-life was delicately skated over in the court proceedings which followed the murder of his mistress. In those days the most extraordinary deference was paid to the aristocracy. The tongues wagged, of course, but no one questioned his lordship's right to do what, in the case of an ordinary mortal, would have been social death in Victorian England.

It is not recorded whether Lord Lucan ever met the formidable Belgian cook who involved him in this embarrassing scandal. It is not likely that it would be more than a passing encounter at No. 13 Park Lane, for the only thing they had in common was a steadfastness under fire.

The gallant old soldier, however, may not have known that his mistress's cook was a battle-scarred veteran of the Commune. The Paris Communards were regarded by the English ruling classes with the same disfavour as were the Revolutionaries of eighty years previously, though many of them were admitted as refugees to England following the atrocities which accompanied their suppression in Paris, during which a conservative estimate of 20,000 men and women were shot when the revolt was finally put down.

Marguerite Diblanc was born at Mex-devant-Virton in Belgium and emigrated to Paris with her parents when she was a child. Nothing is known of her early years, or how she became mixed up with the Communards. It was more likely that she became associated with them because they happened to be her friends than because of any political convictions on her part. And many firm and passionate friendships were made during those terrible days in Paris in 1871, which were in many ways worse than the Terror of the previous century.

Marguerite was a hefty, masculine girl of twenty-eight. *The Times* described her : " Her complexion is clear, her mouth large and sensual. The nostrils are slightly dilated. She has cold blue eyes. Her forehead is low but broad and her hair is thick. Her neck and shoulders are powerful. Her hands, which she tries to conceal behind the folds of her skirt, are those of a man."

She came to London with the refugees of 1871 and got a position with a M. Eugène Dumas, who owned a well known pork butcher's business in Soho. She later became cook to Mme. Riel.

The Riel house, for a Park Lane establishment, would seem to have been understaffed by the standards of the period, for there was only one other servant, apart from Marguerite, a not very bright maid by the name of Eliza Watts.

Eliza's natural dimness was further accentuated by the fact that the Riel household was entirely French-speaking. Neither mother nor daughter spoke much English, and communication with Eliza was mostly by signs.

Mme. Riel was the most difficult and exacting of mistresses. Eliza seemed to endure her all right, and anyway understood very little of the Gallic abuse which was poured upon her. But with Marguerite it was different, and her independent spirit soon brought her into violent conflict with her mistress.

There were frequent rows and arguments. Mme. Riel discussed the matter of the cook with her daughter, and on 21st March 1872, Julie sacked Marguerite and gave her a week's wages.

This caused another row. Marguerite had been paid monthly and rightly considered she should have had a month's wages, despite the fact that Julie said it was the French custom never to give a servant more than a week's wages on dismissal. Eventually the Riels agreed that Marguerite should work for another month and then go.

This didn't really satisfy Marguerite, who wanted the month's money. She was not happy in England and wanted to return to Paris, now at peace again, and where her friends were. But Mme. Riel had no more intention of giving her a month's money than her daughter had, so the conflict in the house between the cook and her employers continued unabated.

On 31st March, Julie Riel went to Paris for a week's holiday before the start of her season at the St. James's, where she was to appear under the management of Raphael Félix in a series of popular French comedies.

The rows, on the evidence of Eliza, who didn't understand what they were all about, continued between Marguerite and Mme. Riel throughout the week.

On Saturday, 6th April, Mme. Riel had a female guest to dinner, after which Eliza put the remains of the food back in the pantry, locked it and gave the key to her mistress. The pantry at 13 Park Lane was always locked in this manner, as Mme. Riel kept her money and jewellery there as well as the food.

The following morning, 7th April, was the usual Sunday morning for Eliza. Up at six, cleaning and sweeping, then breakfast in bed for madame at 9.30. Just after eleven, Mme. Riel was dressed, and told Eliza she was going for a short walk in Green Park with the dog, and that she was later expecting a friend who was to be told to wait. Mme. Riel went downstairs with the dog, while Eliza continued her work in the upper part of the house.

Before she went out, Mme. Riel went down to the kitchen where she found that Marguerite had not yet begun preparations for the day's cooking. She demanded to know why the soup was not on to boil.

Marguerite replied that as the meal was not until seven that evening there was plenty of time. Mme. Riel instantly flared up and there was another violent row, ending with Mme. Riel ordering Marguerite out of the house. Marguerite told her she would be pleased to go, but would not do so until she was paid what was owing to her.

Mme. Riel replied by calling her a rude name and telling her that she could stop if she liked, but she would make her suffer for it.

Marguerite then thoroughly lost her temper and went for her mistress, grabbing her by the throat and there was a struggle.

The two women parted and continued the slanging match. Mme. Riel again ordered Marguerite from the house, and told her she would have to go on the streets, which was the proper place for her.

Marguerite wasn't going to take this from someone she well knew was only a kept woman. She told her pointedly that she would not be so long on the streets as Mme. Riel had been.

This insult caused more blows to be struck. It was not surprising that the older and more portly Mme. Riel decidedly got the worst of the fight with the brawny Marguerite.

Mme. Riel picked up a saucepan and came for Marguerite to hit her with it. But Marguerite got in first and punched her on the point of the jaw. Mme. Riel fell backwards on the kitchen floor and did not move again.

73

Marguerite—this is her story—believed that she had killed her, though it was possible that Mme. Riel was not dead then.

Marguerite heard signs that Eliza was coming down from the upper regions, so she dragged Mme. Riel's body out of the kitchen, across the area and into the coal cellar, and locked the cellar door.

Eliza, meanwhile, had come down and found to her surprise that the dog was still on the stairs. She went down to the basement. Marguerite came in from the cellar with some coal, saying that the cellar was now empty of coal.

Eliza remarked that it was strange that Mme. Riel should go out and leave the dog behind. But even if Marguerite fully understood what Eliza said, Eliza certainly did not understand Marguerite's reply.

It was essential now to get Eliza out of the house for a while, as Marguerite could not leave Mme. Riel's body in the cellar, so she sent Eliza, jug in hand, to get some beer from a near by public house. As soon as she had gone, Marguerite locked the doors of the house and returned to the cellar.

She found Mme. Riel's body difficult to move, so she got a rope which she tied around the waist and started to drag it into the kitchen. She still found the body difficult to move as it kept doubling up in the middle, so she untied the cord and fixed it around the neck. She was able to make some progress now, though, despite her strength, it was a laborious business.

She started to haul the body in this fashion up the stairs, which led directly from the kitchen up into the pantry.

Meanwhile, Eliza had returned, and was knocking on the door, impatient and indignant at being locked out.

Marguerite hurriedly pulled the body, still hauling it head first with the rope around the neck, into the pantry, the key of which she found on her victim's chain.

If Mme. Riel had been alive when Marguerite dragged her into the coal cellar, she was certainly dead now from strangulation by the rope. The medical science of the day was not exact enough to be able to tell precisely which of the many injuries had caused death.

Having left her mistress's body on the pantry floor, Marguerite

74

placed her mantle on top of it, and then, with Eliza still banging impatiently on the door outside, Marguerite turned her attention to finding the money which was due to her and which would enable her to escape from the country before the body was discovered.

She found the safe unlocked and she opened it and found there a number of five-pound notes and some sovereigns. She helped herself, well aware, of course, that she was taking very much more than was due to her. But the temptation was too great. There was also a locked strong box in the safe which she knew contained Mme. Riel's jewellery but, although the key to this was on her mistress's chain, she did not attempt to open it.

Eliza was still hammering on the door and it was time to go. She left the safe door open, but she closed and locked the pantry door, and went down to admit the indignant Eliza. Marguerite ignored her angry protests at being locked out, avoiding an explanation as usual by taking refuge in the language difficulty.

They then had lunch together. The afternoon was spent by Marguerite in preparing for her flight, and she was easily able to conceal such preparations as she made from the dim-witted Eliza. Marguerite knew she would have to be away that night, for madame's daughter, Julie, was expected back from Paris in the morning. She was travelling on the night boat.

During the afternoon, a Mme. Crosnier, the visitor Mme. Riel had told Eliza she was expecting, called. Eliza took her to Mme. Riel's room where she waited for three hours, finally leaving, puzzled at her friend's absence, as well as the maid's inability to account for it.

About six o'clock Marguerite changed into her best green satin dress, telling Eliza she was going to church. Eliza said she would not go with her, for the mistress would be very angry if she returned to find her out. Meanwhile, she had found Mme. Riel's gloves in the kitchen, and asked Marguerite how they came to be there, a question which Marguerite evaded as she did all the others.

Marguerite did not leave the house until nearly eight o'clock and told Eliza she would be back by ten.

Marguerite now hurried down Park Lane and into Piccadilly

where she hailed a cab and told the cabby, John Turner, to take her to Victoria. At the station they had an argument over the fare, which was a shilling, Marguerite wanting to pay him ninepence. The misunderstanding was due more to the language difficulty than anything else, for Marguerite did not want to draw attention to herself, which she unfailingly did, owing to her difficulty in making herself understood.

At Victoria she attracted more attention by having an argument over her ticket to Paris, which was finally sorted out by a clerk-interpreter named Werner. She had apparently wanted a cheap ticket, and he told her she would have to wait until morning for a cheap train to Paris. She finally bought a first-class ticket on the night boat-train, which cost her £3, which she paid for with a five-pound note. Werner got the guard to put her on the 8.20 train.

And so Marguerite made her escape to Paris.

Meanwhile, Eliza was waiting at 13 Park Lane for the return of her mistress and the cook. When neither had returned by midnight, she went to bed.

Her incuriousness about her mistress's absence was perhaps not surprising. Undoubtedly she thought that Mme. Riel was on one of her periodical visits to 36 South Street to wait upon the diminishing desires of her noble patron.

Eliza was up early on the Monday morning, knowing that Mlle. Riel was due back from Paris on the night boat. The first thing Eliza noticed was that Marguerite was still absent. She looked into Mme. Riel's room and found that her bed had not been slept in either.

She was not much disturbed by this situation. She knew that Marguerite Diblanc was under notice, and that it was not the first time that her mistress had been absent for a whole night. Her staff knew very well in whose bed she may have slept.

That was the first thing that occurred to Julie Riel when she arrived in the company of Mme. Gedde, one of her mother's friends, from Victoria just after seven o'clock that morning to find her mother not at home. She cut short Eliza's rather confused account of the mysterious happenings of the previous day and promptly sent her round to 36 South Street to see if Mme.

76

Riel was there. Eliza was told at the Lucan establishment that her mistress had not been there.

Julie obviously had reason to doubt that her mother had slept with Lord Lucan that night. She thought she might have left a message, so she and Mme. Gedde searched the house together. They found nothing, and eventually came to the pantry. Julie, who had her own key, opened it.

She saw on the floor what looked like a heap of clothing, on the top of which was her mother's mantle. When she came closer, she saw to her horror that the heap was her mother's dead body.

She immediately summoned Dr. William Wadham, of St. George's Hospital, who lived at No. 12 Park Lane, while Mme. Gedde called in a passing constable.

Both the doctor and the constable inspected the body. The latter observed that it was lying on its face and knees. The rope was still around the neck, and one end of the rope was twisted around the safe door, which was open.

The doctor was able to establish at once that it could not have been suicide, and that death had taken place not in the pantry but somewhere else.

The hunt was immediately on for the missing cook, and when Julie found about eighty pounds missing from the safe, the motive was obvious.

Inspector Pay investigated the case. He found fishbones and coaldust in the dead woman's hair and coal marks on her clothes. In the coal cellar he found one of the dead woman's hairpins. It was an easy guess that Marguerite Diblanc would return to the Continent where she had friends, and the Inspector's inquiries soon uncovered the evidence of the cabby John Turner, and the clerk-interpreter Werner, both of whom remembered their encounter with the foreign woman answering the description supplied by Inspector Pay.

The next day Scotland Yard sent a telegram to Paris:

London, April 9th, 1871.

To: M. Claude, Chief of Paris Detective Force.

Marguerite Diblanc woman accused of murder Belgian

77

aged 28 height five foot four inches round full face ruddy complexion thick brown hair green satin dress dark grey waterproof black velvet cap with large pendant rose. In her possession French bonds and five-pound Bank of England notes. This woman left London on Sunday by London Chatham and Dover mail train for Paris with first-class ticket number 4856. Please seek and if possible arrest her—Williamson.

In the meantime a certain Mme. Victoire Bouillon of 192 rue St. Denis, Paris, had received a letter from England which read :

April 6th.

My dear Victoire—If you have not written, do not write. I leave this evening for Paris. No, do not expect me, perhaps I shall never see Paris, nor even my parents again. I will try to leave for America and if I arrive there I will give you my address. So, *adieu*, my dear Victoire, and think of me often. I finish by kissing you with all my heart. Your devoted friend, Marguerite Diblanc.

This rather touching letter is an important piece of evidence. The murder—if murder it was—took place on 7th April. Now Marguerite's letter, dated the previous day, suggests premeditation. In which case Mme. Riel was certainly murdered. Marguerite, however, said that she wrote the letter on the afternoon of the 7th and mis-dated it. The fact that the letter was post-marked the 8th supports this. In which case it was manslaughter.

Marguerite arrived at Mme. Bouillon's house on the 8th, despite the fact that her letter suggested that she was not to expect her. Perhaps she changed her mind. Perhaps she found it more difficult to go to America than she had thought, though with £80 in her possession she would not have found it difficult to pay the fare across the Atlantic, and there were no passport and visa difficulties in those days. The New World still opened its doors to all who wished to go.

Jacques Bouillon was a silver-plate worker. His wife Victoire and Marguerite came from the same village in Belgium. The

Bouillons had known Marguerite since she was a child. Before the recent war with Prussia, Marguerite had lodged with them, and had left owing them money. She now repaid them what she owed.

Marguerite stayed two nights with the Bouillons, and on the morning of the 11th she went to stay with a fellow Belgian, Thomas Gérard, who was a coal merchant, of 18 rue du Porte St. Denis. Gérard also knew Marguerite's family.

Marguerite confessed the whole story to Gérard and told him of her desire to escape to America. But Gérard immediately betrayed her to the Paris police who were now looking for her and who promptly arrested her. Gérard's treachery may have been due to a desire to keep in with the police owing to his former Communard sympathies.

The Bouillons were more loyal and did their best to prevent the police getting evidence against her. But the police not only found the green dress mentioned in the Scotland Yard telegram and the letter to Victoire, but also Mme. Riel's purse and keys and some of the stolen money.

The Bouillons were thereupon arrested and charged with receiving stolen property.

Meanwhile, there was plenty of free speculation about the case in the English Press. The *Pall Mall Gazette* inclined to the view that Marguerite was really a man, in view of her rather masculine appearance and the violent nature of the crime, and that " he " was now living in the Paris underworld.

So far Lord Lucan's name had been kept out of it, except for an oblique reference at the inquest to 36 South Street, but he could not have been in much doubt that the storm was about to burst around his head.

The inquest on Mme. Riel was held in the Mount Street Workhouse on 10th April. The jury first of all visited the scene of the crime.

Julie Riel in her evidence said her mother was 42, though later she was stated to be 46. She was the widow of Jules William Riel of independent means. After her father's death, her mother had not remarried. Julie naturally made no reference to their

79

benefactor, and she did not seem to think that her mother's relationship with the old cavalry general was in any way disreputable. But then Julie was an actress and the stage was not a respectable profession in Victorian eyes. Julie herself was not a Victorian. Parisiennes of the nineteenth century were not influenced by the prudery which characterised English society in those days.

Dr. Wadham had conducted a post-mortem on the remains. He told the coroner that he found heavy indentations on the neck caused by the rope, and many bruises on the face, as well as minor injuries. He found the vessels of the membranes, the lungs, kidneys and liver gorged with blood. The hyoid bone and two of the neck cartilages were fractured. He considered death was due to strangulation.

Eliza gave evidence and it was she who first mentioned going to 36 South Street, though the coroner was discreet enough not to press her to state who lived there.

The jury returned a verdict of wilful murder against Marguerite Diblanc.

Although the Paris police had Marguerite in custody, Scotland Yard had great difficulty in extraditing her.

The French raised an interesting point. Under the extradition treaty, the French reserved the right to try their own nationals, even though the crime was not committed in France. This right still exists under French law.

Everyone knew that if Marguerite Diblanc was tried in France for killing her cantankerous mistress during a violent quarrel, she would run no risk of being executed, and the French police indeed told her that. But if she was tried in England, she would stand a very good chance of being hanged. It is reasonable to believe therefore that the obstructions the French government put to extradicting her were based on humane grounds. English law has not a very good reputation for humanity, then or now. Certainly during the early part of the nineteenth century, English justice was one of the most inhuman of any in the civilised world.

The English now held that Marguerite was a Belgian, and therefore could not be tried in France as a French subject. Paris then suggested that Marguerite might have become naturalised in Lorraine which had since the 1870 war been ceded to Germany; and anyway, if she was Belgian, the Belgian government would have to consent to extradition. As Belgium had abolished capital punishment, it was not thought her consent would be forthcoming.

However, for diplomatic reasons, Belgium raised no objection to the extradition, but the French still prevaricated. It was not until the end of April that Marguerite was finally brought back to England by Inspector Pay, and after various diversions to avoid the crowds of sightseers, she was brought to King Street police station, Westminster, and charged with murder.

On 1st May, she appeared before a magistrate, Sir Thomas Henry. With him sitting on the Bench as curious spectators, sharing the same mentality as the vulgar mob outside, were several distinguished members of the aristocracy who included Lord Sandys, Viscount Macduff (who later married into the Royal family), Marquess Townshend, Viscount Ashley (the future Earl of Shaftesbury) and General Lord George Paget, who was second-in-command of the Light Brigade at Balaclava, and distinguished himself in the famous charge.

Mr. Harry Poland opened the case for the Crown and called Eliza Watts who told her story of what happened at 13 Park Lane on the Sunday of her mistress's death.

Julie Riel then told of the finding of her mother's body. She said that before she left for Paris, she gave her mother £30 in five-pound notes. This money, together with her mother's keys and purse, was missing after Mme. Riel's death. She had gone to Paris on 12th April and identified some of the missing articles.

Mr. A. S. Godfrey, the defending solicitor, cross-examined her with the obvious intention of involving Lord Lucan in the case. He first asked her if she knew whether there had been a man staying in the house while she had been in Paris, but the magistrate disallowed the question.

Mr. Godfrey then asked Julie about the £30. Whose was it? Julie replied that it belonged to her mother. Where had she got it from? Julie then provided the expected sensation by saying that Lord Lucan had given it to her.

The eager public had to wait until the next day to see the celebrated general go into the witness box to explain his financial arrangements with the murdered woman. Some of the five-pound notes paid out on his behalf on 30th March had been found in the possession of Mme. Bouillon.

He said that he remembered handing six five-pound notes to Julie Riel to give to her mother, for whom he said he had undertaken to cash a dividend warrant as she had no banking account herself. The matter was left, with the air full of unanswered questions, such as how was it that a lady without a banking account came to be living at such an opulent address, and who indeed was paying her rent?

Marguerite's trial took place at the Old Bailey on 12th and 13th June. The Bouillons and Thomas Gérard had been brought over from Paris to give evidence against her. So much for the loyalty of her friends and compatriots.

Poor Marguerite indeed stood alone, with the peculiar English judicial procedure loaded heavily against her for, as the law then stood, she was not allowed to give evidence on her own behalf. She had no chance to tell her story.

The prosecution could call all the other participants in the affair to give evidence against her, but the defence were forbidden to put her into the witness box to defend herself against the murder accusation.

Upon such insubstantial ground is the myth of the superiority of British justice founded. It was no wonder the French were reluctant to deliver her up to the fickle mercy of the English courts.

As for the Bouillons, they may indeed have been under intolerable pressure from the police. Jacques Bouillon said of Marguerite, that though he had always thought she was of an amiable disposition, she was passionate when thwarted, but for all that she had a good heart.

Marguerite's own story could only be elicited from witnesses such as Gérard, to whom she had told it, and who was anyway a hostile witness. The defence had to do their best in cross-examination to present Marguerite's point of view. This strange state of affairs persisted in English courts until 1898, and it was only because most juries were wiser than the legal minds who framed the laws that there were not more miscarriages of justice in the nineteenth century.

The star turn of Marguerite Diblanc's trial was, of course, the Earl of Lucan, who had to give evidence about his murdered mistress before a crowded and intensely curious court.

All his life he had been in the public eye, and his actions subjected to fierce criticisms—from his harsh treatment of his Irish tenants during the famine, to his stubborn incompetence as the cavalry commander in the Crimea. He had since lived down the hatred and vilification. But never before had he been subjected to the kind of sniggering which greeted this uncomfortable revelation about his private life.

All the same, the court treated him with deference, and he did not have to undergo the kind of cross-examination which a man, whoever he was, would have to endure in such circumstances today.

He was asked questions about Mme. Riel's manner towards other people. He protested to having seen Mme. Riel only occasionally, upon the accuracy of which statement he was not pressed. He said he had not had the opportunity of observing her behaviour with other people. Like many French ladies, she had a lively quality, and although she was hasty, he had never known her to lose her temper.

His former mistress's bad temper was a fact too well established to be ignored, but the old general evaded the Attorney General's searching questions about it with more skill than he displayed on the field of battle twenty years previously.

Marguerite's counsel was able only to call evidence as to character, but he made a strong and moving plea on her behalf. Here was a woman in a foreign land, unable to speak the language, or understand half of what was going on in the court—although her very life depended on it.

He did not deny that the prisoner had killed her mistress, but she had not done it wilfully and she had had great provocation. Mme. Riel's temper was well known. Her treatment of the prisoner had been unbearable. She had never been able to keep servants, and was always finding fault with them and using strong and irritating language. The prisoner had wished to leave, but in a strange land had not known where to go. Her mistress had refused to pay her her due, nor would she let her go. Moreover, she had insulted her intolerably by telling her she could go on the streets. The infuriated Marguerite had then attacked her mistress with all the power of a strong woman whose feelings had been outraged. The jury might think there had been no intent to murder.

As for her taking the money, it was established that she did not know the value of the notes, and she had taken what she thought was due to her, and simply to facilitate her escape after such a dreadful calamity. She had left behind her far more valuable property than she had taken. As for the letter to Victoire Bouillon, counsel did not think that the jury would have any doubt in deciding that it was written after the calamity and that the prisoner had dated it in error.

Two of Marguerite's former employers, one of them M. Dumas, the Soho pork butcher, gave her a good character. Each said she was honest, and not in any way violent.

Both the Attorney General and the Judge made much of the legal point of verbal provocation, and the Judge ruled that in law words alone were insufficient provocation to reduce the crime of killing to manslaughter.

After such a direction, the jury could return no other verdict but guilty of murder, although they added, a little to the judge's annoyance perhaps, a rider saying that premeditation had not been proved and that they strongly recommended her to mercy.

When asked if there was any reason why the death sentence should not be passed on her, Marguerite replied in French: " I never had the intention to cause death."

She turned pale when the grim words of the death sentence were translated to her.

The judge told her: " The jury have felt themselves called upon, in consideration of the grounds they have stated, to recommend you to the merciful consideration of the Crown. It will be my duty immediately to forward that recommendation to the proper quarter."

The jury were undoubtedly affected by the statement in court by a French police inspector that the crime in his country would not carry the death penalty.

The jury's tacit admission that English justice was harsh, was plainly not shared by the judge, nor the editor of *The Times* who, as was his custom, pontificated on the case afterwards. " We hope it will not be hastily assumed that murderers who have acted under the impulse of sudden and violent passion have a claim to mercy."

Marguerite was sentenced to death on 13th June, but she had to wait in the death cell until 21st June before hearing that she had been reprieved. The reprieve may well have had something to do with the attitude the French adopted towards the case.

It is not known how long Marguerite was in prison, or what happened to her afterwards.

No such obscurity engulfed the third Earl of Lucan. Five years after the trial, his Countess died, but the old war-horse himself lived on into his eighties. In 1886, he was appointed Gold Stick in Waiting, and the following year, at the age of eighty-seven, was made the oldest Field Marshal in English military history. In 1888, vigorous and alert to the last, he died at the age of eighty-eight.

Some students of the case think that Marguerite was lucky to have escaped the hangman, and have compared her with the infamous Kate Webster, another formidable servant, who literally butchered her mistress at Richmond, Surrey, in 1879. After first hacking her to death with an axe, she dismembered her body on the scullery floor, pausing half way through her gruesome task to go to the local for refreshment, then returning to boil her mistress's remains in the kitchen copper. Later she was said to have sold two jars of the remains to the publican as " best dripping ". She was hanged on 29th July 1879.

Kate—a thirty-year-old Irish woman—was supreme in her class, and Marguerite Diblanc is in no way to be compared with her.

Marguerite was almost certainly a lesbian, though personally she may not have been a very interesting character. But her

85

life touched some of the great events of her day, and she certainly made a ripple of sensation across the placid mid-Victorian scene.

Jeanette Edmonds
(1871)

THE BEST corrective for thinking that the Victorian age was dull is to browse through the yellowing pages of the newspapers of the day, all carefully preserved in the British Museum's Newspaper Library at Colindale.

While the back numbers of *Punch* provide a valuable clue as to how the middle-class Victorians spoke and what they joked about, the files of the *Daily News* and *The Times* will tell you how they behaved, if you apply a certain amount of imagination to the reports of those extraordinary and sensational *causes célèbres* which were printed at great length in their columns.

Judging by their newspapers, the Victorians were as avid readers of sex and murder scandals as we are today. Cases were reported in great detail and with a marked lack of inhibition in the nineteenth century.

From some of these reports those long-dead Victorians spring to life in startling fashion, and their doings certainly give the lie to the belief that English home life in the 'sixties and 'seventies was fashioned upon that of their revered Queen. Nor does one discover that the Victorian girls were all shy retiring violets who would not look at a piano leg and would shudder at the thought of sex.

For instance, there was Jeanette Edmonds, a very formidable and extremely good-looking girl of twenty-two, who in 1871, deliberately set off a highly explosive sex and murder scandal in the sleepy Gloucestershire town of Newent, which had the whole country by the ears.

Jeanette was no retiring Victorian maiden. She was indeed no maiden. But then, she was hardly living in a typical Victorian household.

Her uncle, Edmund Edmonds, was the local Newent solicitor, and although his establishment had all the trappings of nineteenth century respectability which his position in the community required, things were not all that they seemed under the Edmonds' roof. It had been going on during the 'forties, 'fifties and 'sixties, but it was not until the 'seventies that the explosion came.

Jeanette's father, Edmund's brother, had died when she was a child, leaving seven children. Her uncle took her into his own house and brought her up and educated her as his own daughter. He had no daughter of his own, but three sons—Edmund, the eldest, Ralph and Oscar.

Despite the terrible battle which eventually took place between Edmonds and his niece, there was undoubtedly a very special relationship between them. They were both formidable people, towering above all the others who took part in the tremendous drama which they finally played out at the Old Bailey. They were both obstinate fighters, and would rather destroy themselves than give in to each other. There must have been a very healthy respect—perhaps a love–hate relationship between them.

After she left school, Jeanette, who was as clever as she was attractive, earned her keep by acting as unpaid secretary to her uncle, who had quite a flourishing practice.

It was not long before Jeanette became aware that the family doctor, Matthew Bass-Smith, was developing an interest in her which was very unprofessional. Jeanette responded with a mixture of caution and coquetry. Dr. Bass-Smith had known her since she was nine or ten. A married man with four children of his own, he took his time over the seduction. She was worth waiting for. He had watched her grow from an awkward child into an extremely attractive and desirable girl, and Bass-Smith decided to seduce and relish her at his leisure.

He was assisted in his design by the fact that he was a friend of the family, and was becoming well aware of the scandalous little secrets which were hidden under the respectable roof of the tall house at Newent.

Edmonds' relationship with his wife was, to begin with, an interesting one.

She was a Miss Ann Matthews, who in 1835 had married a Mr. R. E. Legge of a wealthy Newent family, who died in 1844 at the age of 36, leaving her pregnant. The child died at the age of four but inherited a substantial legacy under the Legge estate.

The Legge family heartily disapproved of Ann, and said the child could not possibly be her husband's as at the time of conception he was half paralysed and incapable owing to his intemperate habits. They tried unsuccessfully to get the money back.

Meanwhile, Edmonds had married Ann. She had apparently written him some letters in which she made it plain that the child was his. These letters fell into the hands of a man named Hollister who promptly started to blackmail Edmonds with them.

Edmonds paid up. He could afford it, and obviously thought it was worth it, as he and his wife were enjoying the proceeds of a legacy to which they were not, strictly speaking, entitled.

He paid blackmail for nine years, and then either Hollister put the price up, or Edmonds decided he had paid enough. Anyway, when the victim refused to pay any more, Hollister promptly made good his threat and sent the letters to the Legge family, which was just what they were waiting for. They immediately brought an action for the return of the dead infant's legacies. This was in November 1855. Edmonds and his wife won the action and kept the legacy, although the judge put it on record that he was satisfied that Edmonds had had sexual relations with his wife before their marriage, which was not a thing people in Victorian times liked having said about them—especially supposedly respectable solicitors in small West of England towns like Newent.

In view of his reputation, which certainly pursued him throughout the 'sixties and into the 'seventies, Edmonds' professional success was perhaps surprising.

But it became obvious, in the far more sensational scandal that followed, that Edmonds couldn't leave women alone, and indeed had a great deal of success with them, much to the chagrin of his now fading wife who during the 'sixties began to have an extremely difficult and troublesome menopause.

And so during these decades the Edmonds' house flourished and increased. Ann Edmonds had given birth to three sons, and Jeanette joined the family. In 1860, Ann's young sister, Mary, also became part of the household and was known to the children as Aunt Polly. She was twenty-eight then, and it was probable that the master of the house had his eye on his sister-in-law right from the start, though one can believe that he hesitated to carry on an intrigue with her in his own house and under his wife's nose. Ann was jealous enough as it was, and he would never have got away with it; and anyway, he had plenty of lady-friends.

The fact that Edmonds' business prospered might well have been something to do with the fact that he concentrated on lady clients. This caused endless trouble with Mrs. Edmonds.

In the early 'sixties she had found a love note from the children's young governess addressed to the master of the house, and the governess was summarily dismissed. Later she complained bitterly about her husband's unprofessional relationships with his lady clients—particularly a Mrs. Smallridge, who lived in Gloucester.

Edmonds had the maddening habit of praising the charms of other women to his wife, whose own charms had become, in her fifties, mere memories.

In 1864 her health began to deteriorate and she developed a congested liver and some kind of heart disease. This, together with her difficult menopause, caused her considerable mental and physical suffering. She was an awkward and querulous invalid, and could not reconcile herself, as many women of the time did, to her husband's philanderings.

By 1867, Mrs. Edmonds looked like settling down to a long period of disagreeable semi-invalidism. She was under the constant attention of Bass-Smith, who could not do much for her anyway. He was more interested in using every opportunity of being in the house to pursue the seduction of Jeanette.

So far she had resisted him. According to her, his first attempts to seduce her started in 1866 when she was seventeen. She held out until the following year, after her aunt's death. We can only guess at the reasons which made her submit.

After all, he was a middle-aged married man of no wealth, and she was an attractive girl with an uncle and aunt of some substance who had to all intents and purposes adopted her. There was no reason for her to suppose that she could not make a good marriage. There was no daughter in the household to compete with her.

Becoming the mistress of a middle-aged married man who was in no position to support her in any way was not a thing a Victorian miss did lightly. It was no step to a marriage of any kind. It was more likely to be the first step to the streets.

Jeanette might or might not have known into what dark waters she would be venturing if she yielded to the lecherous family doctor. Whatever might have been going on behind the façade, it was certain that Jeanette was subjected to the stern moral training which all young girls of her time went through.

She no doubt had more than a vague knowledge of her uncle's philanderings, for her aunt was always loudly complaining about them. But she was aware that that sort of thing was allowed in the man's world and that the double system of morality was loaded heavily in their favour—as indeed it still is.

Jeanette could not avoid hearing the bitter quarrels between her aunt and uncle which were always over other women.

She might even have been aware of the case which had been brought against her uncle and aunt all those years ago. Her uncle, as a legal man, would doubtless have kept records of the case of Legge *v.* Edmonds, 1855, and as his secretary, she might have found it fascinating reading to have discovered that her highly respectable aunt had committed adultery with Uncle Edmund while she was married to her first husband and had had an illegitimate child. Certainly the details of the case were well known locally. Edmonds went out of his way to mention it at the inquest on his wife in 1872.

Anyway, whatever Jeanette's thoughts and intentions were as she parried the advances of the lustful doctor, she retained her virginity until after the death of her aunt, a terrible event in the house, after which nothing was the same again in the family.

The death of Mrs. Edmonds on the night of Sunday, 24th February 1867, was a mystery never to be satisfactorily solved. The occupants of the house subsequently told different stories, but as it was not until 1872, five years later, that they were asked to recollect what had happened, it was not entirely surprising that there was some discrepancy in their stories.

Jeanette was in her eighteenth year at the time. There had been the usual quarrels over Uncle Edmund's lady-friends, but the atmosphere improved temporarily during that Sunday evening when some friends came to supper and stayed to a musical evening. Sacred music was sung and Mrs. Edmonds had obliged with a portentous piece called *Too Late, Too Late* !

Mrs. Edmonds certainly appeared in good health and spirits on the last evening of her life. The guests left about eleven, after which Mr. and Mrs. Edmonds had a violent row in the break-fast room about Mrs. Smallridge, which was heard by several other members of the household.

There is evidence, too, that Edmonds became violent and started throwing things.

A little later, Mrs. Edmonds came upstairs to her sister's room, collapsed and said she was dying. The doctor was sent for.

Bass-Smith found her insensible and sinking. There was nothing he could do for her and she died at twenty-to-one on the morning of the 25th.

Mrs. Edmonds' death caused a great convulsion in the family, and a lot of awkward questions were asked, for the servants had all heard the uproar which preceded their mistress's sudden and unaccountable death. Newent was abuzz with rumour.

Bass-Smith saved his friend Edmonds a great deal of embarrassment by signing the death certificate without any question. It was a good thing to get Edmonds into his debt in view of his own lust for Jeanette, and Bass-Smith had his plans all worked out.

He had not failed to notice the way Edmonds eyed his young

and still quite shapely sister-in-law. With Ann out of the way, Bass-Smith, who knew all about his friend's philanderings, guessed that Mary Matthews would soon take her sister's place in Edmonds' marital bed—not officially, of course, for the law permitting a man to marry his deceased wife's sister was not passed until 1907.

Bass-Smith knew how to play on this situation, without telling Edmonds anything about his carnal intentions towards Jeanette. It would never do for Edmonds to know, for whatever immorality went on behind the façade of respectability, the outward conventions must be maintained. Edmonds was a family man and a stern father. He was always laying down the laws of morality and propriety to his children, and the fact that he disregarded them himself in his own private life did not make any difference.

Whatever her two younger sons might have thought of their mother—their feelings might be judged by their later behaviour—the eldest son, Edmund, was devoted to her. He was at Cambridge when she died and he rushed home immediately.

His feeling of natural distress at his mother's death was soured and embittered when he heard the stories which were circulating around Newent.

His Uncle James—Mrs. Edmonds' brother—had arrived in Newent for the funeral, but what he had heard of her death so disturbed him that he announced his intention of not attending the ceremony.

Young Edmund certainly went to his mother's funeral, and afterwards he had a violent quarrel with his father, accusing him of being responsible for his mother's death. There was almost certainly no suggestion of murder at this point, but of ill-treatment which hastened her end.

All reports agree that Mrs. Edmonds had become an exasperating and impossible woman, though Edmonds himself was not much better and deliberately antagonised her over his various *amours*. It should be borne in mind, too, that, with her death, Edmonds was now in full control of the legacy their bastard son had wrongfully inherited from the Legge estate.

It seems that only Edmund was on Mrs. Edmonds' side. The

quarrel between father and son went so deep that it caused an irreparable breach between them. Edmonds himself was outraged that his son should question him.

Young Edmund's university career was terminated, and he left for Australia. We don't know when he left the country, but if the evidence given later on in the trial is to be believed, it was some months after his mother's death.

All the family, except the eldest son, had sided with Edmonds over the controversy, and for various reasons.

Family unity is a powerful thing. A family will unite against the world in order to protect itself, regardless of right or wrong. For this reason, crimes are frequently concealed by families, who prefer to have secrets, however grim, rather than endure the odium and publicity which the process of justice entails. It is when the family splits and quarrels that these secrets come out. In the view of the family, there is often no point in attempting to bring one of its members to justice, not because justice is fickle, which it is, but because most families think the intrusion of justice only makes matters worse from the family's point of view.

Certainly all the members of Edmonds' family, with the exception of his eldest son, rallied round him. They did not want the scandal and embarrassment of an inquiry into the circumstances of Mrs. Edmonds' death.

It was certainly in the interests of all of them to protect the head of the house, without whom there would be no comfortable home, and it cannot be denied that they were all, Jeanette included, looking after their own interests.

Several interesting and noteworthy things happened shortly after the funeral.

On 11th March, Jeanette wrote a letter to her widowed mother which said among other things: " Dear aunt appeared no worse than usual during the day. About eleven o'clock she was going to bed as usual and as was her custom went to Aunt Polly's room to talk, when she was suddenly seized by apoplexy and in less than an hour had breathed her last. She was very happy after death . . . I have indeed lost my best friend."

Jeanette said that this letter was written at the instigation of Aunt Polly who was at her elbow when she wrote it. And the recipient, Jeanette's mother, who was financially dependent upon Edmonds' generosity, was careful to preserve it.

It can hardly be doubted that the guiding spirit behind this and other judicious precautions taken just after Mrs. Edmonds' death, was the legal mind of Edmonds himself. He took several prudent steps to insure his future. A hint to Jeanette's mother about preserving the letter would be quite sufficient.

He also took certain precautions about the servants whom he employed at the time of his wife's death. His domestic staff consisted of three maids—Ann Bradd, Mary Ann Mills and Ann Cassidy—and a coachman, John Arch. Edmonds remained in touch with all of them, except Ann Bradd, after they had left his service, and regularly sent them presents.

Ann Cassidy subsequently married the coachman, who changed his job, becoming a railway signalman. All the same, Edmonds did not lose sight of them and Aunt Polly always sent them Christmas hampers. Later Edmonds was able to summon them quickly to come and give evidence on his behalf.

Ann Bradd was the only awkward one. She was in Mary Matthews' room during Mrs. Edmonds' death scene and saw what had happened. She said that she was told to say nothing about what she had seen.

Three weeks after Mrs. Edmonds' death, Mrs. Matthews, Mrs. Edmonds' mother, questioned Ann Bradd about her daughter's death. Mrs. Matthews, from all accounts, did not get anything much out of Ann Bradd, apart from the rather lurid story that she had heard her mistress's death rattle while she was in the kitchen making gruel, which was a sheer invention.

Mrs. Matthews, said the servant, offered her hundreds of pounds if she would say what really happened, but Ann Bradd refused to be bribed, saying she had promised Miss Matthews she would say nothing.

Six months later she had a row with her master and was dismissed. She told him he was a bad man and would come to a bad end.

Seeing that old Mrs. Matthews' suspicions had been aroused about her daughter's death, one wonders what sort of account she managed to get out of her younger daughter, who had now taken her sister's place as mistress of the house. Mrs. Matthews must have been very dissatisfied with her daughter's replies, or she would not have turned to a servant for information on such a matter.

The position of Mary Matthews—Aunt Polly, as the children called her—is worth considering more fully, for she may well have been the key to this curiously interesting drama which was really only just beginning with her sister's death.

Mary Matthews had every reason to conceal what was going on behind the heavy curtains of the tall house at Newent, every reason to protect her brother-in-law, and even, putting her in the best possible light, to shield his two young sons, Oscar and Ralph, from the odium and scandal which the truth might bring upon them.

She was thirty-five, not a glamorous age in the nineteenth century, though she must have been attractive in a mature kind of way. She was placed in an awkward position. Supposing she denounced her brother-in-law, what was to happen to her? And to the children, for whom she obviously had some affection? She knew no other home but this. If it was wrecked, she would be lost too.

Supposing Edmonds, in a moment of intolerable provocation, had struck his wife, after which she had had some kind of fit and died? This surely was just a ghastly accident, and in the interests of everyone it was wisest to hush it up.

There is little doubt that Edmonds was strongly pressing this point of view upon his sister-in-law in the dark and desperate hours of the night of Ann Edmonds' death, when the terrified children had been finally hushed to sleep and the house was wrapped in gloom and horror. And it seemed to her the only way out of an appalling situation.

And she loyally and devotedly stuck by the bargain she made.

However one might criticise this rather interesting Victorian spinster, one must admire her unswerving loyalty.

What followed the death of Mrs. Edmonds was in some ways worse than what preceded it.

Nothing is certain, for the sordid little secrets were denied and covered up in a desperate attempt to maintain the Victorian façade of morality. The only one in the house who spoke was Jeanette and her motives at the time were certainly open to question.

Jeanette swore that Aunt Polly became her uncle's mistress shortly after the death of Mrs. Edmonds, and she told the Newent magistrates' court in February 1872, that Aunt Polly had a miscarriage in 1869 and that " she washed her linen ", to quote the *London Daily News* of that date.

Jeanette was not the only one who suspected intimacy between Edmonds and his sister-in-law, both of whom were to deny it publicly. It was a terrible thing to be accused of in those days. But today, though we may deplore their hypocrisy, we might regard their intimacy with leniency.

Mary Matthews may well have been in love with her personable and successful brother-in-law, whom the state of the law forbade her to marry. After all, she was the mistress of the house and her great dread must have been that he would marry again, when she would be supplanted and almost certainly have to leave the house. Then where indeed would she go, for she had no means of her own?

Who could blame her for doing everything in her power to keep Edmonds to herself, and preventing him marrying again? She probably exercised a more sensible toleration towards his lady-friends than her sister did.

Less forgivable was her undoubted toleration of the seduction of Jeanette which finally took place within a year of Mrs. Edmonds' death. But Aunt Polly was put into a very difficult position over this, and how could she resist the diabolical blackmail which Bass-Smith now brought to bear upon her?

Bass-Smith, the family doctor, probably more than Edmonds himself, was the evil genius of this disreputable slice of Victorian life. His lust for Jeanette's young body was his consuming passion. She was eighteen now and he was over fifty.

It would be wronging the man to say that it was purely a physical fancy on his part. There was good reason to believe that he genuinely cared for her, and their love affair lasted for at least four years.

What made Jeanette finally give into him and yield him her body? This can only be guessed. The mid-Victorian girl, of course, had far less chance of meeting men than her modern counterpart. Life was much less interesting. There were long, boring evenings. Excursions into Gloucester to the concert, or perhaps even the theatre, were rare, and she was, of course, always chaperoned.

For all this, Jeanette probably had less scruple than her contemporaries, and it could not be said that she was living in the usual high moral Victorian surroundings. She knew about her late aunt's carryings on with Uncle Edmund before they were married, resulting in an illegitimate child; and now she knew that Aunt Polly had become Uncle Edmund's mistress, and with Aunt Annie only just cold in her grave too.

She certainly had no shining example to follow, especially with her mind haunted by the manner in which Aunt Annie had met her death.

It was not to be supposed that she was a frightened, fluttering virgin when Bass-Smith seduced her. Virgin she may well have been, but she almost certainly went into it with her eyes wide open. Jeanette was no innocent little fool.

One brief description of her has been handed down to posterity. It was written by the *Daily News* reporter who was at the inquest on Ann Edmonds on 14th February 1872. " She was handsome, prepossessing, and she gave her evidence with great coolness."

Jeanette showed every sign of feeling quite romantic about her middle-age seducer. She called him Antonio and he called her Cleopatra.

The intimacy with Bass-Smith prompted Jeanette to open her heart to him about what had happened on the night of her aunt's death. He had always entertained suspicions about it, of course, and was well aware of the lurid stories which were being told in the neighbourhood. He had signed the death certificate without question, more as an act of friendship than anything else.

He had no intention of going back on that, just then, anyway. But he had every intention of using it to further his affair with Jeanette, for having successfully seduced her, he wanted to continue the affair. But this had its dangers, for his friend Edmonds must not know.

This was where Aunt Polly came in. Bass-Smith knew her weak spot well enough and he proceeded to work on it and to blackmail her.

He knew by now that she dreaded the revelations which he and Jeanette could put before a shocked and startled world. It was as much in Aunt Polly's interests to keep certain things quiet as it was in her brother-in-law's, for she was now fully committed with him, if not much in love with him.

What Aunt Polly's reaction was when she heard of Jeanette's seduction will never be known, for she subsequently denied in the most strenuous terms that she knew anything about it.

But the weight of evidence was against her. The doctor spent whole nights in Jeanette's bed, and even if the master of the house was a heavy sleeper, it is not to be supposed that anything of that kind went on under his roof without Aunt Polly knowing about it.

At the times when Bass-Smith was a guest in the house, it was easy for him to go to Jeanette's room at nights. At other times, after he had spent the evening with Edmonds, he left his host at bedtime, then returned to the back door, where Aunt Polly let him in.

Time and time again, according to the pair of them, Aunt Polly facilitated their nights of love in this fashion, and the conclusion is irresistible that Bass-Smith was able to exert a blackmailing pressure upon Aunt Polly. Jeanette's silence was not difficult to secure, so long as she was under Edmonds' roof and enjoying his bounty. But Bass-Smith's silence had to be bought, and it is reasonable to suppose that Aunt Polly was just as afraid to tell her brother-in-law what was going on as the doctor himself was. For Aunt Polly to be having an affair with Edmonds, well, in view of the circumstances, and the fact that the law would not let them get married, there was some excuse for that.

But the eighteen-year-old Jeanette with the fifty-year-old

family doctor—that was different. It would shock a lot of people today, let alone a hundred years ago.

The person who appeared to have taken the situation the least seriously was Jeanette herself. This young lady took a decidedly romantic view of her middle-aged lover, and later on was coolly and unashamedly announcing to the scandalised Victorian world that she was the mistress of a married man with four children and old enough to be her father.

But if we find Jeanette a puzzle, we are a little blinded by a false view of the nineteenth century. The 'sixties and the 'seventies were times of great intellectual stirrings and revolutionary ideas. Not only was there Darwin and Karl Marx and a great upsurge of atheism and republicanism in England, but women's rights and women's freedom were being strongly preached, and free love was being discussed, particularly by a women's faction in New York led by Victoria Woodhull, who practised it openly and unashamedly.

Jeanette was certainly well abreast of her times, but her boldness did not extend to telling her formidable uncle what was going on. She knew better than to court trouble from that direction.

She concealed the affair very successfully from him. She said she once spent three nights with Bass-Smith at an inn at Kenilworth, telling her uncle she was staying with a Mr. and Mrs. Docker at Brewood; and on that occasion she had taken brazen pleasure in sending her uncle a letter of birthday greetings—writing it practically, as it were, from her bed of shame.

There was little doubt that Jeanette enjoyed being Bass-Smith's mistress. Reprobate he unquestionably was, but there must have been something attractive about the old scoundrel to have held a girl like Jeanette for four years. She evinced no shame at being a fallen woman. There is evidence, too, that she had Bass-Smith round her little finger.

In all the riot of illicit sex that went on so secretly and discreetly behind the heavy curtains of the respectable solicitor's house at Newent, there is never any suggestion that Jeanette ever found herself embarrassed by an unwanted pregnancy, although it seems that Aunt Polly was less fortunate in this respect. Probably the doctor knew a thing or two which the solicitor didn't.

Jeanette suggested that Aunt Polly had to perform an abortion upon herself in 1869. It was typical of the age that the unfortunate lady could not call upon the medical knowledge of her fellow conspirator in the love nest, who could have made things considerably easier for her.

It should be remembered, too, that while all this was going on there were two growing schoolboys in the house, Ralph and Oscar. Was it possible that the protagonists in all this irregular coupling managed to conceal it from this pair of inquisitive boys? Perhaps and perhaps not. Whether the boys knew or not, they were very much under their father's thumb, and, despite the later rift, there was no suggestion of any real antagonism towards Jeanette.

However well the couples got on together, Bass-Smith and Edmonds, after a while, fell out with each other. This was nothing to do with their secret sex life. They fell out, as so many people do, over money. Bass-Smith apparently owed the solicitor £586 and on the other side of the ledger there was some argument about Bass-Smith's medical fees which the solicitor had not paid.

The fact is they fell out. The doctor no longer came to the house and his encounters with his attractive young mistress became fewer. Then he moved to London where he became a partner in a practice.

The two lovers now continued their affair by correspondence, which seems to suggest that it was still burning brightly even after four years. Secret letters, smouldering with passion and sprinkled with indiscretions, passed between them.

On the 8th of October, 1871, one such letter which Jeanette was in the middle of writing, fell into her uncle's hands. A highly indiscreet passage ended with the suggestion that the good doctor, anonymously referred to as usual as Antonio, might have her stays made as would best suit his amorous convenience.

Edmonds was appalled at such tacit confession of immorality as the letter contained, and there was a tremendous explosion. Perhaps when she recollected Uncle Edmund's own conduct in such matters, Jeanette could not resist a smile when he stormed at her, calling her a strumpet, a wicked unprincipled hussy, and all the traditional epithets in the Victorian book.

Her impertinent smile earned her a violent smack across the face, and she was promptly ordered out of the house and told not to return.

Edmonds had not yet discovered who " Antonio " was, and the spirited Jeanette compounded her offence by refusing to tell him. Aunt Polly, of course, knew, but she wisely kept out of it.

Jeanette did not leave until the following morning. She had no money and was not allowed to take her luggage. The unfortunate girl was indeed in something of a fix. It was no use going to her uncle asking him for money in his present mood. He intimated she could go on the streets for all he cared, which was indeed a more suitable place for her than his house.

The irony and hypocrisy of the situation may not have been lost on Jeanette; and anyway she scorned to ask him for money.

Nor apparently did she approach Aunt Polly, or if she did she had no success. In any case, that lady sided with her brother-in-law in all things, and was not prepared to risk his displeasure, although she must have felt some responsibility for the situation herself.

It was Ralph, the second son, who had recently left school, and who was now old enough to be something of an admirer of his attractive cousin, even if he disapproved of her morals, who lent her the money to make her journey—thirty-seven shillings, to be exact.

No doubt the humiliation of being turned out of the house in this fashion burned into Jeanette's soul as she walked to Newent station that October morning in 1871. She may even then have been planning her revenge—a revenge which was destined to bring ruin to them all, including her lover and herself.

She first went to some friends in Gloucester, then on to her mother's at Newport. But she wasn't very welcome there. Her mother was having a struggle to support her brood of fatherless children and was much dependent on Edmonds for financial help. She didn't want to offend him.

Jeanette then sent for Bass-Smith, who came immediately and collected her from her mother's. He took her to London, spending the night with her *en route* at a hotel in Leckhampton, one of their favourite amorous rendezvous of the past.

He took her then to his home in London. But with his wife and children there, her position was a little difficult. But the pair of them were used to disguising their true relationship, and it is not to be supposed that they had much difficulty under the nose of Mrs. Bass-Smith.

But it was not a situation which could last, so after a few days she wrote to the vicar of Newent, the Rev. Keene, for help, and he came to London and secured her admission to a Home for Fallen Women at Hammersmith. We are not told how Jeanette fared in this formidable Victorian establishment which was no doubt run practically on penal lines.

But the Rev. Keene's interest in her was not without an ulterior motive. Was it usual for West of England clergymen in the nineteenth century to rush all the way to London—more than a hundred miles—to rescue a fallen parishioner? Of course not. Jeanette was someone very special. He knew all about the rumours concerning the late Mrs. Edmonds, and he was eager for justice to be done to the memory of his late-lamented and ill-used communicant—for she had been a regular churchgoer. And now here, with a big grudge against her uncle, was Jeanette, who knew well enough what had taken place in the house that February night in 1867.

Jeanette herself was only too anxious to set off the train of fire which would lead to the long-anticipated explosion. She had already discussed the matter with her lover. She told the vicar the whole story.

Her uncle, she declared, had murdered his wife.

In the meantime, Jeanette had asked Bass-Smith to return to Newent and demand her boxes. This he did and when he and Edmonds faced each other, there was an almighty row, as was only to be expected, for Edmonds then realised that this man, who for years he had welcomed into his home as a friend as well as family physician, had shockingly abused his friendship and hospitality. In blistering terms, Edmonds bitterly reproached his former friend for seducing Jeanette and he refused to let him have her boxes.

103

In a rather curious turn of phrase, the unabashed doctor replied: "So long as I have a feather to fly with, I will have Jeanette." To this Edmonds replied that he would not have her for long, though what he meant by this is not clear, unless he had a reconciliation with the girl in mind. It is not to be supposed that he had no regard or affection for her, or that he was not missing his unpaid secretary. And perhaps the thought of his wife's death was still uppermost in his mind. He did not want Jeanette to make trouble. Perhaps by now the wicked hussy had learnt her lesson. Who knows what was in his mind?

But he had no time or patience with the girl's seducer. If Jeanette had come to him, it might have been different, and the story might have ended there, with tears, contrition and an avuncular forgiveness. For whatever might be said against Edmonds, he was not a mean or a hard man, and he treated his relatives with considerable generosity. Jeanette was to him the daughter he should have had, and he must have had considerable affection for her, despite everything. But Jeanette was proud, unbending, the same as he was. They were two obstinate spirits now setting out to destroy each other. Their situation was the very stuff of the highest human drama.

When Edmonds still refused to give up Jeanette's belongings, Bass-Smith threatened that he would create such a stir in Newent "that the dead would rise from their graves".

Edmonds knew what the threat referred to, but was confident that he could not only call Bass-Smith's bluff, but would bring retribution on him for what he had done to Jeanette.

The first thing he did was to try and get Bass-Smith struck off the medical register for gross unprofessional conduct with a patient. Then he issued a writ for the £586. Bass-Smith promptly filed his petition in bankruptcy, which was just as promptly opposed by Edmonds.

Bass-Smith then threatened to rake up the old story about Mrs. Edmonds' death and, when Edmonds ignored the threat, Bass-Smith informed the Gloucester coroner that he wished to revoke the death certificate he issued for Mrs. Edmonds in 1867, as he now had reason to believe that the circumstances of her death required investigation.

The Rev. Mr. Keene had also been to the coroner with Jeanette's story, but some time elapsed before the storm, which had
been pent up for four years, burst.

Newent was a small town, and the feeling against Edmonds
had been smouldering ever since his wife's mysterious death. The
local authorities themselves do not seem to have been impartial
in the matter. Jeanette left her uncle's house in October, and
later that year was in the Home for Fallen Women at Hammersmith. It was not until the following year that the authorities
took action.

Edmonds himself hoped right up to the last minute to make
Jeanette change her mind. Jeanette's sister, Mary, paid a somewhat mysterious visit to her sister a few days before the inquest.
Mary was on her uncle's side and the inference is irresistible that
she went to try and make Jeanette change her mind from a
course which would ruin the whole family—not only Uncle Edmund, Aunt Polly, Oscar and Ralph, but Jeanette's own mother
and brothers and sisters.

Jeanette herself, of course, was already ruined. Nothing could
alter that.

But Jeanette was deaf to this plea. She persisted in her allegations. She repeated them to the coroner and in consequence he
ordered Mrs. Edmonds' body to be exhumed.

Edmonds, the prudent, far-sighted legal mind, seeing what was
about to happen, then put his well-laid plans into operation, and
began to assemble his witnesses and see that their stories all coincided. Former servants were brought from far and wide and
lodged in his house. They were all well disposed to him, remembering those Christmas hampers. His own family were carefully
coached in what they were to say. He was going to take no
chances.

It was at this point, in mid-February 1872, that the story
burst for the first time upon the outside world, and the newspapers were full of it.

Mrs. Edmonds had been laid to rest in a beautiful tomb of
white marble, lovingly inscribed in Latin. This was pulled apart
and the body was taken out. The *Daily News* said: " The
coroner and the jury viewed the body in its dissected condition

in the vestry in the presence of the husband and others interested."

Whether such primitive pathology—in the vestry of all places —served any useful purpose is doubtful. But it certainly stirred up the anti-Edmonds feeling which flourished in the Newent district, and fed the morbid curiosity of the newspaper readers of the day. Juries of those days must have had strong stomachs to witness such macabre evidence.

The coroner opened his inquest on 14th February and it lasted for three days.

The star witness was Jeanette, whose looks and personality obviously caused something of an impression.

Her story was that, following the quarrel which took place between her uncle and aunt on the night of the latter's death on 24th February 1867, her aunt came running out of the back dining-room screaming, and up the stairs into Aunt Polly's room, followed by her uncle who was in a state of great passion. Her aunt crouched away from him in terror on the far side of the bed.

Jeanette went to her and she said, " Oh, Jeanette, I am dying —I am dying."

Her uncle was still in a terrible rage and Aunt Polly was trying to restrain him.

He said to his wife : " You be damned! You be damned!" She had replied : " It is not I who will be damned, but you."

That enraged her uncle so much, said Jeanette, that he rushed over to his wife and hit her violently on the head with his fist.

" Aunt Annie sank on the floor after that and never spoke again," said Jeanette. " I tried to undo her dress, but could not as she was so swollen. After I gave her water she put her hands to her head several times. When Uncle Edmund approached Aunt Annie again, I tried to bar his path, thinking he was going to strike her again, but he brushed me aside. He did not hit her again. And then we sent for Dr. Bass-Smith."

When the doctor came, continued Jeanette, he asked the dying woman what she had had for supper, but he was unable to do anything for her.

Jeanette said nothing to the doctor at the time about the violent scene which preceded her aunt's death, though she had often discussed it with Aunt Polly—who, with Ann Bradd, also witnessed what had happened.

Jeanette told the coroner that she was shocked and disgusted with her uncle because she knew he had murdered his wife, but she had never spoken to him about it. When asked why not, she said it was because she was afraid of him.

Jeanette unashamedly admitted that she had been the doctor's mistress for four years, that Bass-Smith had seduced her after her aunt's death, and shortly after her seduction she told him what had happened that night. Bass-Smith had said to her: " Your uncle is a worse man than I am. If he exposes me, I will expose him."

Jeanette, herself revealed to the world as an unrepentant fallen woman, told the story of her seduction in such a manner as to put Aunt Polly in the worst possible light. Not only did she connive at it in order to keep Jeanette and the doctor quiet about the subject of Aunt Annie's death, but Aunt Polly herself had an immoral relationship with Uncle Edmund. Jeanette had seen her going into her uncle's bedroom when everyone was thought to be asleep.

The effect that these revelations had upon a small community like Newent, already ill-disposed towards Edmonds, can be imagined.

Jeanette's story about her aunt's death was corroborated by Ann Bradd and Dr. Bass-Smith, who said it could certainly have accounted for the condition of the dying woman when he arrived, for Mrs. Edmonds had a weak heart.

Edmonds himself gave evidence at the inquest. He was not permitted to at his trial, owing to the state of the law as it existed then.

He said that his wife's health had seriously deteriorated during the last year of her life. On the night of her death he had been planning to go to London on business, but his wife was pressing him to stay owing to her health. There may have been an argument, but he insisted there was no quarrel.

She preceded him upstairs and went into the room where her

sister and Oscar, the youngest son, slept. It was there that she said she was dying and looked as though she was going to faint. He went for the doctor who bled her but could not save her life. He denied that he struck his wife or swore at her. He denied that he had had sexual relations with his wife's sister, Mary. He also took the opportunity to deny that he had had sexual relations with his wife before they were married. This, of course, had nothing to do with the matter the coroner was inquiring into, but Edmonds knew it had been common talk in Newent ever since the Legge case in 1855. Memories are long in the west country.

Edmonds' story was borne out by Aunt Polly and his two sons and several of his former servants. Despite this, the jury found that Mrs. Edmonds had died of apoplexy, and that her death had been accelerated by violence on the part of her husband. The coroner accordingly committed him for trial on a charge of manslaughter.

This was on the 16th February. On the 19th the local magistrates considered the evidence and committed Edmonds to the Assizes on a charge of murder, and, as is usual in such cases, refused him bail. It was at the magistrates' court that Jeanette told the story of Aunt Polly's miscarriage.

The local "justices" must have shared very strongly the popular feeling against Edmonds. While there may have been a case for manslaughter, there was certainly no *prima facie* case for murder on such evidence as was heard by the Bench. Murder is unlawful killing with malice aforethought. There was no evidence of premeditation or the use of any lethal weapon. The Newent magistrates were as biased against Edmonds as were most other people in the district. The charge on which they committed him was " feloniously killing and slaying his wife ".

Between 19th February, when Edmonds was committed, and 8th May, when his trial began, plenty of things happened.

Edmonds himself was indefatigable. He was not a man of the law for nothing. The first thing he did was to apply for bail.

It is not entirely without precedent for a person charged with murder to be granted bail, though it is certainly unusual. After considerable legal argument, the application was granted by Mr.

Justice Hannen, who no doubt took into consideration the fact that the coroner's jury thought the charge should be manslaughter and not murder. He granted Edmonds bail in his own surety of £4,000 and in two or four sureties of the same amount at the discretion of the magistrates, who being nettled at the judge's implied criticism of them, made the bail as stiff as possible.

Edmonds, now released from prison, set about organising his defence with characteristic vigour and thoroughness.

On 19th March, he applied to Mr. Justice Willes for his trial to be moved from Gloucestershire Assizes to the Old Bailey in view of the local prejudice against him. He did not think he would get justice in Gloucestershire.

There was plenty of evidence of prejudice. The vicar of Newent, who had been in the forefront of the movement to bring Edmonds to justice, and who had encouraged Jeanette to give evidence against her uncle, had preached a very indiscreet sermon on the day before the magistrates' hearing, using such expressions as "horrible revelations", for which he publicly apologised in a letter to *The Times* (27 March 1872).

Edmonds also complained of the disparaging attitude of the local Press, of prejudice on the part of the local Bench in committing him for murder in the teeth of a manslaughter finding by the coroner's jury. Some malicious doggerel, unfortunately not reported, said to be circulating in Gloucestershire, was read to the court.

As for the Rev. Mr. Keene's indiscreet sermon, Mr. Justice Willes pointed out to him the dangers of choosing his text from contemporary events. Were there not enough examples of vice and virtue to be found in the pages of Holy Writ?

The judge decided there was local prejudice and ordered the trial to take place at the Old Bailey.

What was Jeanette doing that spring while waiting to take the stage at the Old Bailey for the final act of the drama? Was she still at that Hammersmith home, or—more likely—were she and Bass-Smith still pursuing their love affair?

Bass-Smith, seducer and scoundrel though he was—and he admitted to it—had not left her in the lurch. When Uncle Edmund threw her out in the street without a penny and just in the clothes she stood up in, Bass-Smith immediately came to her aid. No doubt he ruined and debauched her, but he was always there when she wanted him. Unlike so many seducers, he didn't just take what he wanted and then leave her.

Their love affair had withstood four difficult, hole-in-the-corner years. They must have been in love with each other, those two.

There is evidence that Jeanette's sister proposed going into business and wanted to take Jeanette in with her—if she would give up Bass-Smith. But Jeanette would not give him up.

As for him, he had had to get out of his practice owing to the publicity the case had brought. His marriage was ruined and his wife divorced him.

To Bass-Smith, Jeanette was still the most desirable girl in the world, despite the fact that she was the most publicised fallen angel of the day. And he wasn't the only one who found her an exceedingly attractive person.

It is not reasonable to suppose that in the circumstances the doctor and his young mistress would have remained apart. They now had nothing to lose in being together openly.

The trial began at the Old Bailey on 8th May, having been postponed from the April sessions. The judge was Baron Bramwell. Mr. Digby Seymour, Q.C., prosecuted, assisted by Dr. Kenealy, Q.C., and Mr. George Griffiths. Edmonds' formidable array of counsel were led by Mr. Huddleston, Q.C., and consisted of Serjeant Parry, Mr. Henry James, Q.C., Mr. Griffiths and Mr. George Browne.

The accused asked if he might sit with his counsel, as he was a solicitor conducting his own case, and it was necessary that he should be in constant communication with his counsel. After some discussion, this rather unusual request was granted.

The first witness was Ann Bradd, who said she had been in service to the Edmonds family from 1864 till August, 1867. On Sunday, 25th February 1867, she heard Edmonds say to his wife: " Go to bed!" Mrs. Edmonds said, " You brute! You wretch! You went to see Mrs. Smallridge." The witness had heard the accused praising the beauty of Mrs. Smallridge at supper. Edmonds said, " Damn your eyes! Go to bed!" Then he threw something at her—something heavy which struck something and then fell to the ground. Mrs. Edmonds screamed dreadfully, then ran out of the door, her arms up, still screaming. She said, " There's a dear man, don't ! " Later the witness heard screaming from the garden. Edmonds later rushed up the stairs. Mrs. Edmonds was in Miss Matthews' bedroom, saying : " I'm dying—I'm dying. Water, water, Jeanette." The witness later took water to her and saw her lying on the side of the bed apparently dying, with Miss Matthews and Dr. Bass-Smith leaning over her. A half an hour later she was dead. The witness had always believed that the thing that had been thrown in the breakfast-room was a candlestick. She had twice been asked to say nothing about the episode. She said nothing about it to the deceased's mother, because she had promised Miss Matthews.

In cross-examination, Ann Bradd admitted that she had been dismissed at a minute's notice the following August, and that she had told her master he was a bad man and would come to a bad end. The first person to speak to her about giving evidence was a police officer, since when she had been staying with a friend at Bridlington.

Huddleston was unable to shake this very important witness, who seemed to have no reason to lie. Servants were often dismissed in those days of prolific domestic labour. The woman had had no difficulty in getting further employment, so it was not likely that she had a grudge against Edmonds—apart from a desire to see justice done to her dead mistress.

Ann Bradd's evidence is vital when considering this case. She was the only domestic present at the scene which led to Mrs. Edmonds' death, and she had told a consistent story to the coroner, the magistrates and the Old Bailey jury. To the coroner she had added that she had frequently heard Edmonds swear at his wife and tell her he wished she was dead. She also had told the coroner that she thought her mistress's death had been due to an unlucky blow given in the height of passion.

The coroner's jury believed her and decided it was manslaughter, but the dolts of the Newent Bench, in their blind prejudice, altered it to murder. This in one sense was as well for Edmonds, for the charge obviously could not be sustained on the evidence, and once the jury had rejected it, he could not be charged on the lesser count of manslaughter.

Ann Bradd concluded in re-examination that she had been in many positions since she left the Edmonds, but the memory of her mistress's last night had always haunted her.

Jeanette Edmonds then told the Old Bailey the same story as she had told the coroner and the magistrates. She now had to undergo the ordeal of cross-examination which was severe, particularly as she had so blatantly defied the moral code of the day.

It should not be thought that Jeanette was the soul of truth. This tarnished Victorian maiden did not want to admit in court that she had been thrown out of her uncle's house because of her affair with the doctor culminating with the letter to Antonio which contained the slightly blue reference to her underwear. She said her uncle turned her out because she made a mistake in a letter. He struck her on the head and told her to leave.

The evidence was against her on this point, though she would not admit it.

This is an extract from her cross-examination by Huddleston, as reported in the *Daily News* of 9th May 1872:

There had been intimate relations at this time between you and Dr. Bass-Smith?—There had.

How long did you carry on an illicit intercourse with Dr. Bass-Smith after your aunt's death?—Four years.

Yes, she knew he was a married man. The doctor was staying in the house as a guest and used to go to her room.

I stopped three days and nights with him at Kenilworth. My uncle thought I was visiting Mr. and Mrs. Docker at Brewood and I wrote him a letter congratulating him on his birthday. (Laughter)

After she left her uncle's, Smith came to see her at her mother's house and took her with him to his own house and she saw his wife.

Later I told the vicar that Mr. Edmonds had killed his wife.

Starr Faithfull

Charlotte Bryant with her third child

Did you say killed or murdered?—Well, murdered, if you like.

This was after your uncle had endeavoured to get your lover removed from the list of surgeons and he had refused to give up your boxes?—Yes.

Why was he to be taken off the list of surgeons—for seducing you?—I suppose so.

Jeanette said, when re-examined by the prosecuting counsel: " In letters after my aunt's death, I only stated what Aunt Polly told me to state about the way she died."

Jeanette did not suffer under cross-examination to the same extent as did Dr. Bass-Smith who was the next witness.

He said that on the night of the alleged murder, Mr. Edmonds came to him and said his wife was in a fit. When he arrived at the house, Mrs. Edmonds was sinking and insensible. " I helped to get her into bed, tried to bleed her in the arm, put crolin oil on her tongue, mustard plaster on the back of her neck. I saw from the first that it was a hopeless case and death took place at 12.40 a.m. I formed the opinion that she died of apoplexy." Miss Matthews said there had been no violence or disturbance.

The fact of a person going upstairs screaming, he said, would be consistent with concussion of the brain. " But I cannot understand how this could have occurred in a case of apoplexy. There must have been a blow to produce it."

Later Edmonds said to him: " I think I killed my wife, through my unkindness—murdered her through my unkindness. I have been a brute and a villain to her."

Speaking of the occasion he called for Jeanette's boxes, he told Huddleston, cross-examining, that Edmonds had shaken his fist at him, but did not call him a villain or a scoundrel.

Mr. Huddleston: Will you tell us any other name more applicable to you than a villain or a scoundrel? (Laughter)

Witness: I don't remember what he called me. He asked me what business I had with Jeanette. I said I took her in and helped her after he, Edmonds, had thrown her out.

H 113

Did you try and seduce this girl before her aunt's death?—
I can't recollect.

Did you continue to have illicit intercourse with her for
years?—I did.

He said he had frequently been up whole nights in the
house with Jeanette and had been let in at the back door by
Aunt Polly time after time. (Laughter)

Bass-Smith denied that he had at any time tried to influence
Jeanette's evidence.

Medical opinion followed. The senior surgeon at Gloucester
Infirmary said he found the remains of the prisoner's wife too
decomposed for him to form any conclusion as to how she died.
There was no trace of any injury to the skull.

Aunt Polly was the last witness of the first day of the trial and
she denied that there was any violent scene on the night of her
sister's death.

In recounting the events of that night, she said she went to
bed after Jeanette and had left her brother-in-law and his wife
downstairs. She shared a room with Oscar, who was ten at the
time. Later, Mrs. Edmonds came into the room to say good
night to Oscar. Edmonds was with her. Mrs. Edmonds had been
trying to dissuade him going to London on account of ill-health,
while Edmonds was suggesting that his wife should accompany
him and they should go on to Cambridge where their eldest son
was being educated. Mrs. Edmonds wouldn't agree to this, and
suddenly she began to feel ill. Jeanette had come in by that time
to say good night. A little later, Mrs. Edmonds collapsed and
said she was dying.

Only the briefest account has come down to us of Aunt Polly's
cross-examination, and we don't know how she fared under the
redoubtable Mr. Digby Seymour. But the scene she describes
seems an unlikely one in certain respects.

In the first place it was late—10.30 or 11.0 p.m. Was it not
odd that Mrs. Edmonds should have gone to her ten-year-old
son's bedside to say good night to him at that late hour?
Secondly, it was obvious that some kind of argument was going
on, or why should Edmonds have followed her into the bedroom

where the boy was sleeping and continued it there? Thirdly, Jeanette presumably had already said good night downstairs. Why come into the room to do so again, if she had not been disturbed by the uproar?

Aunt Polly, of course, denied everything that was in the least incriminating to her brother-in-law, or which would cast any reflection upon the propriety of their household. She said she knew nothing of Jeanette's seduction by the doctor until the compromising letter was found, and she denied with outraged scorn any suggestion of immorality between herself and her brother-in-law.

On the second day of the trial the defence witnesses went into the box one after the other to deny Jeanette's story. The burden of their evidence was the same—there was no quarrel, no screaming, no blows were struck by the prisoner.

The members of the family who gave evidence were Edmonds' two young sons, Oscar and Ralph, and Mary Edmonds, Jeanette's sister, who had visited her at Hammersmith and who had offered to start a business with Jeanette if she would give up Bass-Smith. They were all dutifully loyal to Edmonds, and Mary was not asked who was to put up the money to start the business.

Several of Edmonds' former domestics and employees gave evidence for him, including Ann Arch, the former Ann Cassidy who married the coachman.

Some of these witnesses were criticised for the alacrity with which they came forward to give evidence for their former master, and were asked if they had been prompted or coached in their evidence. They all seemed to know the right answers to that, but the court were a little sceptical about them. Edmonds, the prudent man of law, had prepared his defence well—perhaps too well.

There was talk in the course of the evidence about a bent brass candlestick and a broken velvet-backed whisk brush, and much ingenuity was displayed by the defence to prove that these articles could not possibly have been used as weapons upon the unfortunate Mrs. Edmonds.

In the summing-up, of course, Bass-Smith, and to a lesser

extent, Jeanette, came in for a fearful lambasting from the long-winded Victorian counsel.

Thundered Huddleston: " No more disgusting admissions than those made by Bass-Smith were ever heard in a court of justice, and it would be a scandal and a disgrace to the administration of justice if the testimony of such a fellow as that had a feather's weight in a case of such vital importance as that before you."

Jeanette did not escape the Huddleston lash: "' Not only is she profligate, but artful and deceitful, and it is impossible to rely on her evidence."

The judge naturally was more temperate and more to the point. He was a little sceptical of all the evidence in view of the length of time which had elapsed since Mrs. Edmonds' death. When people who had always known the truth came forward so late in the day it always excited suspicion.

Dealing with the evidence, the judge said that Jeanette had quarrelled with her uncle and had a motive, that of revenge, for telling untruths about what happened. But Ann Bradd had no such motive. He discounted Oscar's evidence as the boy might have wished to screen his father. The judge found it difficult to believe that a blow was struck upstairs. Though what happened downstairs, no one saw. Could the deceased wife's sister have not only failed to resent a blow being struck in her presence, but continued to live in the house with her brother-in-law?

Baron Bramwell made it perfectly plain that, although he was not satisfied of the prisoner's innocence, the case for his guilt had not been made out beyond doubt.

The jury accepted this and, in less than fifteen minutes, found him not guilty and he was discharged.

In those days the newspapers did not write background stories to sensational cases, nor were the protagonists later paid large sums of money to write their stories for the Sunday papers. Instead *The Times* indulged in an unctuous little homily on the sinful goings-on which it had been reporting at length.

The chief characters of this fascinating Victorian drama—the obstinate, redoubtable solicitor, his faithful, devoted sister-in-

law, the amorous, middle-aged doctor, and the intriguing Jeanette, having all but destroyed themselves in public, then walked
out of the Old Bailey into oblivion.

Ellen Turner

(1826)

THE KIDNAPPING of heiresses by young bloods, who charmed or cajoled them into marriage, was not considered an unusual or unworthy way for a young man in Regency times to get on in the world and increase his fortune.

In American law, kidnapping means forcible abduction and detention in order to exact money, and it is a very serious offence. In England, kidnapping is taking a person to another country against his will. The American style of kidnapping is rare enough in England to be discounted. Here abduction is the more common crime.

Abduction is the forcible or unlawful removal of a person. The Offences against the Person Act, 1861, made it a felony to abduct a female with the intention that she shall marry or have non-matrimonial sexual intercourse, or with the intention of possessing her property. Parliament as usual was a little late, for, by 1861, that sort of abduction had gone out of fashion. Nowadays it is minors who are abducted, and the Act fully covered that particular crime.

This Act was passed a year before the death of a man who had become a distinguished British colonial statesman, and who in his youth had perpetrated one of the most sensational and in many ways heartless abductions of Regency times.

Edward Gibbon Wakefield, judging him by his later life, was the most unlikely man to appear in the blood-drenched pages of the *Newgate Calendar*. There was nothing bloody or monstrous about the crime he committed.

Ellen Turner, the girl he abducted, was cruelly deceived and tricked by him, but after it was over she did at least retain that greatest prize of English girlhood—her virginity. She had, of course, been abducted by a gentleman, and considering that her family were newly rich, it was, in the curiously snobbish opinion of that time, considered rather surprising that they pressed the prosecution against Wakefield. Maybe the rugged Northerners in those days were not quite so enchanted with the aristocracy, or as convinced of their divine rights, as the historians and novelists of the time would have us believe.

Perhaps it was as well for the Commonwealth that Wakefield was prosecuted by this indignant upstart family, for something happened in Newgate which completely changed the life of this young Regency buck. The horrors of early nineteenth-century prison life went deep into his soul and he came out a transformed man, purified by the fires of Newgate.

Edward Gibbon Wakefield was certainly a more interesting person than Ellen Turner. Coming of a good Quaker family, he was related to Gibbon the historian, and Elizabeth Fry the prison reformer, and claimed descent from Edward I. His grandmother came from one of the only two English families which can trace their genealogies to before the Norman conquest.

In a world in which a man was nothing without birth or money, Wakefield's breeding was his most important asset. He acquired more worthy ones in Newgate, but that is a different story.

Wakefield's father was a successful surveyor and land agent and he had four sons—Edward Gibbon, William, Daniel and Arthur. William also played his part in the strange story of Ellen Turner's abduction—and William was dogged by a greater tragedy than was his elder brother.

Edward went to Westminster School. In 1813 he was admitted to the Bar. As he was barely seventeen at the time, the legal qualifications necessary for being called to the Bar in those days cannot have been very high. The following year he became aide to the British envoy at Turin, and spent the next two years, which included the Hundred Days of 1815, in Italy.

In 1816 he was in England, and he eloped with a seventeen-year-old heiress, Eliza Pattle, whose father, a wealthy Canton merchant, had just died.

Women easily fell in love with the fascinating Edward. Eliza certainly did. They were married in Edinburgh, and Edward soon charmed Eliza's mother into recognising the marriage and agreeing to a marriage settlement which was generously to Edward's advantage. He was to have the income for life on an investment of £70,000, which brought him in £2,500 a year— worth several times more than such a sum would be today. Considering that his father-in-law's estate was worth about £160,000, he can be considered to have done very well out of it.

The Wakefields lived for four years in sunny Italy, where Edward was attached to the British Legation at Turin. Italy was not unified till 1860, and in those days Turin was the capital of the Kingdom of Sardinia.

Wakefield was in clover, with a respectable income at last, living the high life in fashionable Italy, waiting for his wife's twenty-first birthday when she would inherit her fortune, and he would be able to get his hands on the capital.

Eliza bore him two children, but she died in 1820, four and a half months before her twenty-first birthday.

The happy days were over. Wakefield's hopes of fortune were dashed. For some years he lived in Paris with his two children, who were being looked after by a Mrs. Phyllida Bathurst, the widow of a British diplomat who took some interest in the Wakefields and their affairs.

His brother William was with him in Paris at this time, pursuing a love affair which was to end in heartbreak and tragedy.

The Wakefields moved in an exclusive cosmopolitan set who called themselves the First Circle in Europe. Paris in the 1820's was one of the world's most exciting capitals. The brilliance of Regency London had faded, and the First Gentleman of Europe had became the fat ageing George IV, who was booed in the streets of his own capital and who hid in his fantastic oriental palace by the sea at Brighton.

High society in England was degenerating into a system of grotesque and vulgar snobbery, from which it was not to recover until the end of the century. It was not to be wondered at that intelligent people had nothing but contempt for a society in which a piece of straw on a lady's petticoat, implying that the wearer had been " forced to resort to a hackney coach, could set a room of fine people tittering."*

To France and Italy went the bright spirits of the age in those first few decades after Waterloo. English society had become a bore. The grace and elegance of the 18th century was destroyed for ever in the English Industrial Revolution. The French Revolution ended the *ancien régime*, but did not destroy elegance or civilised society.

In 1822, Wakefield senior remarried. Edward's stepmother was a lively lady, Frances Davies, daughter of Dr. Davies, a Macclesfield schoolmaster of some standing. She was to play a very important part in the scandal which was to blight their lives.

Her Macclesfield associations were important, too.

In 1825, events were moving quickly which would lead to the abduction of the pretty young daughter of the High Sheriff of Cheshire.

Apart from Ellen herself, the principals in the drama were Edward, his brother William, and his stepmother Frances. In the background, aiding and abetting, was the opportunist Phyllida Bathurst. " Little did I think," she wrote to William, " that when we laughed with Miss Davies [Frances] about Miss Turner, and I desired her to get her for you or him, that Edward would in two or three days' time woo, wed and carry her off.†

The unfortunate William played a rather reluctant part in his brother's abduction plan.

William wanted to marry another heiress, Emily Shelley-Sidney, related to the poet Shelley, and Edward, the born fixer —look how well he did for himself with the Pattles—was in the middle of negotiating a favourable marriage settlement with the girl's father, Sir John Shelley-Sidney, Bart. William was so keen on this marriage that he was prepared to go into this mad exploit

---

* *The Age of Elegance*, by Arthur Bryant (Collins, 1950).
† *Edward Gibbon Wakefield* by Paul Blomfield (Longmans, 1960).

with Edward, and not leave his side while the vital negotiations were pending.

Frances Wakefield undoubtedly knew Ellen Turner. They lived in the same county. William Turner of Shrigley Hall, had just become the High Sheriff of Cheshire in the teeth of the opposition of the local gentry. The Turners had the disadvantage of being new rich and no one was respected in nineteenth-century English society unless their wealth had been in the family for at least three generations. Even impoverished aristocrats had a thin time of it socially and had to reline the family coffers by prudent marriages. To make one's money or earn one's living was a shameful thing.

Turner wasn't a very rich man by the standards of the time, but his capital brought him in about £5,000 a year—worth a great deal more than such an income would be today. Ellen was his only daughter and was not only his heir, but that of his brother Robert as well. She was quite a prize for the fortune-seeking bucks of Regency times, and Edward Gibbon Wakefield was unquestionably one of these.

Ellen was fifteen. He was exactly twice her age.

It was Frances Wakefield who first suggested Ellen Turner as a good match for her step-son, and in this was strongly endorsed by Mrs. Bathurst, who like most widows was something of a matchmaker, and was working behind the scenes to bring about the Shelley-Sidney match for William.

Edward later claimed to have met Ellen at a ball some time before the abduction and to have fallen in love with her. Though Ellen denied she had ever met him until the day of her abduction at the Albion Hotel, Manchester, it may well have been true that Edward saw her at a county ball, for in February 1826 he and his brother were in Macclesfield.

It was on this visit, says the *Newgate Calendar*, that the Wakefield brothers " learned the situation, the wealth and beauty of Miss Turner ". It was certain that Frances Wakefield was in on the plot from the beginning and Phyllida Bathurst was shouting encouragement from the sidelines.

" A more audacious rape of a second Helen no Paris ever undertook," wrote this incorrigible letter-writer. " But he is born for odd adventures and certainly had he been a general would have carried everything by *des coups de main*."

Edward, staying with his brother and stepmother at Dr. Davies' house at Macclesfield, certainly put in some intensive reconnaissance as he carefully laid the plans for the abduction plot.

Shrigley Hall lies about four miles to the north of Macclesfield on the first slopes of the rising Peak country, and the three conspirators rode out to the Hall, visiting the grounds and getting to know all about the Turner family and their doings. The activities of the people in the big house were common talk in the near-by village of Bollington.

Frances herself was of valuable assistance in planning the " odd adventure ", and providing the background material for Edward to perpetrate his heartless deception upon the innocent young victim. Frances got to know Mr. Grimsditch, the Turners' lawyer, and probed him about Mr. Turner's affairs and movements, and Mrs. Turner's state of health, the circumstances of which were to play an important part in the abduction plans.

The " odd adventure " started for Ellen Turner on the morning of Tuesday, 7th March 1826. She was a boarder at a school near Liverpool run by the Misses Daulby—five sisters, Margaret, Phoebe, Elizabeth, Anne and Catherine.

At eight o'clock that morning a green carriage was driven up to the school and a manservant delivered a note addressed to the principal, Miss Daulby, which read :

Shrigley, Monday night, half-past twelve

Madam—I write to you by the desire of Mrs. Turner of Shrigley, who has been seized with a sudden and dangerous attack of paralysis. Mr. Turner is unfortunately from home, but has been sent for, and Mrs. Turner wishes to see her daughter immediately. A steady servant will take this letter and my carriage to you to fetch Miss Turner, and I beg that no time may be lost in her departure, as though I do not think that Mrs. Turner is in immediate danger, it is possible she may soon become incapable of recognising anyone. Mrs. Turner particularly wishes that her daughter may not be informed of the extent of her danger as, without this precaution,

123

Miss Turner might be very anxious on the journey; and this house is so crowded and in such confusion and alarm, that Mrs. Turner does not wish anyone to accompany her daughter. The servant is instructed not to let the boys drive too fast, as Miss T. is rather fearful in a carriage. I am, madam, your obedient servant,

John Ainsworth, M.D.

The best thing to say to Miss T. is that Mrs. T. wishes to have her daughter home rather sooner, for the approaching removal to the new house, and the servant is instructed to give no other reason in case Miss Turner should ask any questions. Mrs. Turner is very anxious that her daughter should not be frightened, and trusts to your judgement to prevent it. She also desires me to add that her sister, or niece, or myself, should they continue unable, will not fail to write to you by post.

Although it was true that Mrs. Turner had had some kind of stroke, this letter was a tissue of lies from start to finish, and it had been rather cleverly composed by Edward. It was in fact something of a masterpiece, and it will be noted that he took every precaution to give an air of authenticity and allay suspicion. The request not to alarm Ellen by telling her that her mother was dangerously ill was astute. Edward was going to have enough difficulty convincing the girl as it was. One can't help thinking that Edward would have made a successful criminal.

The letter was certainly authentic enough to convince both mistress and pupil, who was promptly instructed to return home at once with the servant in the green coach.

When she saw the servant, Ellen expressed surprise at not recognising him. But the man—he was Edward's own servant, named Thévenot—was ready with an explanation. He said her father had recently engaged him as a butler in the new family house. He added that the carriage would return by way of Manchester, where they would pick up Dr. Hull, the Turners' family doctor, and then continue to Shrigley.

Edward had certainly done his homework on the subject of

the Turners' background—in modern parlance, he had cased the job thoroughly—and Ellen was completely convinced and deceived. The fact that Thévenot was a Frenchman helped to convince her, for foreign servants were much sought after by the wealthy and fashionable.

So she stepped into the green carriage, all innocence, and was driven away from school into the most romantic and exciting adventure of her tragically short life.

When the carriage got to Manchester, instead of going to Dr. Hull's house, it stopped at the Albion Hotel in Piccadilly. It was raining, and the hotelier, Robert Wilson, conducted the now slightly puzzled girl to a private suite.

After waiting a few minutes, she was astonished when the most elegant and handsome young man she had ever seen in her life presented himself to her.

Dressed as always in the height of Regency fashion, Edward Gibbon Wakefield was a splendid and formidable figure of a dandy. Brightly coloured coats and brass and gold buttons were, by the decree of Beau Brummell, now out of fashion, and Wakefield was in the dark suit of superb quality cloth and impeccably tailored, a wide-brimmed hat, a spotless white starched cravat, exquisitely cut coat worn open to display a rose-coloured embroidered waistcoat, and a snow-white embroidered cambric shirt, skintight pantaloons with a wasp's waist, jewelled fobs, spotless gloves, white thorn cane, elegant and wonderfully gleaming boots.

These splendid London dandies were little more than a legend to Ellen Turner. They were not often seen in Manchester. She was quite taken aback by his dashing and gorgeous appearance, and overcome by the magnetism of a powerful personality which she immediately felt. Edward was no brainless popinjay, like so many of his kind. He had a keen mind, a good wit and great intelligence.

Ellen was immediately aware of something of this. All the same, remembering the proprieties, she was about to retire from the room when he told her that her father had sent him.

Ellen was fascinated. What girl of fifteen would not have been? Right from the first moment she fell utterly under the

Wakefield spell. He immediately engaged her in an easy and lively conversation and, for his part, was surprised to find that this very attractive child instantly responded in quite sparkling fashion to his wit and sophistication. He had expected a dull provincial Northerner behind that pretty face, and was agreeably surprised to find that she was an accomplished conversationalist despite her tender years, and had a delicious sense of humour.

This instant mutual attraction might well have explained the hectic events of the next few days. Ellen was fascinated by this intriguing stranger. He magnetised her from the first moment.

Edward explained that he was there to take her straightway to her father, and then introduced his brother William, who was there also to escort her.

What poor William thought of this mad escapade we don't know. He was eating his heart out for love of his Emily, now in Paris with Mrs. Bathurst, and he was only here because Edward was on the point of fixing up his ill-starred marriage with the difficult Shelley-Sidney family. And this crazy exploit with Ellen Turner was to cost him everything that he held dear in life.

Having charmed the highly susceptible Ellen into a state of gay co-operation, Edward ordered post horses to be got ready and they went out of the hotel to the green carriage, with the eyes of the staff upon them. Edward knew they would be remembered. He stood out like a gorgeous butterfly in the drab Manchester morning.

Edward handed the girl into the carriage with a gallant flourish, got in with her, while William joined Thévenot on the box and the equipage rolled off down Piccadilly.

Inside the carriage Edward lowered the blinds and continued the business of fascinating his young and willing victim.

" Do you know why you have been sent for from school?" he asked.

" Yes," she replied. " Miss Daulby told me, though she was asked not to tell me that my mother is ill."

He told her that there was a motive for deceiving Miss Daulby. He hinted that the real reason for taking her from school was that there was a sudden change in her father's affairs, which it wasn't desirable that the school should know about, and there was perhaps a way in which she could materially help.

Unscrupulously this man of the world wove his web of lies and deceit around his innocent and trusting young victim. No doubt he did so with some pricking of conscience, for he himself was captivated by her.

Later he confessed—and there is no reason to doubt that he meant it : " Instead of having to bring my conversation down to the capacity of an ordinary schoolgirl, I found that I could talk at random, and that she understood every word I said. She, too, was gratified to discover that I enjoyed her display of a natural wit and a keen sense of the ridiculous with which she is gifted. Marriages, it is said, are made in heaven. Ours was made in the first two hours of our conversation."

The green coach rolled on, taking the road to Huddersfield, where Edward assured her they would catch up with her father who was about on urgent business. They crossed the moors into Yorkshire, with the horses puffing and blowing as they toiled up over Standedge. Then the long descent to Marsden, with the valley not yet scarred by the railway or the great Standedge tunnel.

There was no sign of Ellen's father at Huddersfield, as they changed horses at the George in St. George's Square.

At the George, the staff noted the gaiety of the young lady who laughed and joked with her elegant and distinguished-looking escorts. They were indeed a party to remember. Edward intended they should be, in order to scotch any suggestion of violence or compulsion which might be made later.

It was now dark. The disappointment at not finding her father at Huddersfield was not acute and was borne bravely by the innocent, trusting girl who could not imagine that she could come to any harm at the hands of such a charming and fascinating travelling companion.

Like all schoolgirls, she was romantic, and she was now in the middle of a real-life romance. It would have spoilt it for her father to have suddenly turned up.

So the journey continued by night with fresh horses hauling

the green coach now northwards to Halifax, then up the long slopes and across the moors and the Pennines again.

Ellen, of course, had no idea they were on their way to Gretna Green. When they changed horses to the sound of the cocks crowing at Kirkby Lonsdale, she was a little tired and anxious— due as much to the fact that they had been travelling day and night as to anything else—and Edward buoyed up her spirits by telling her that he expected her father to be at Kendal.

Edward now began to put on the pressure and build up the act. His victim was tired and a little dispirited, though she still responded to the potent Wakefield charm, and he decided to press home his advantage.

His brother was also completely under his influence, and, despite his misgivings, loyally played his part in the cruel deception of this innocent and trusting schoolgirl.

At Kendal they stopped at the Woolpack and the two brothers went into the inn, leaving the girl in the carriage. They came out of the inn with a letter which Edward read standing by the carriage window while his brother looked over his shoulder. They told her that her father had gone on to Carlisle.

After a change of horses and some refreshment, they continued the journey northwards, still on the mythical pursuit of the elusive Mr. Turner.

Ellen's questions could now no longer be brushed aside, and during the long pull up to the Shap, Edward told her the following fantastic story which she seems to have swallowed easily. It was a time of financial troubles and bank failures, and Ellen knew enough about the world to be aware of them. She knew that another schoolfriend of hers had been taken from school owing to a change in her parents' circumstances. When Edward told her that her father had been ruined, she knew it was a thing that could and did often happen.

The bank of Daintry and Kyle at Macclesfield had failed, said Edward, and an uncle of his, who was a banker at Kendal, had lent her father £60,000, which had partially relieved him, though he had had to give Shrigley Hall as security. But now a Blackburn bank had also failed and this had made things worse

Valerie Storie two years after the A6 murder

Where the killer struck on the A6 : Deadman's Hill near Bedford

than ever. Her father was completely ruined, and Edward was doing his best to save his fortunes.

Mr. Grimsditch had hit on a plan which could solve the family's financial troubles. But it was a plan which Edward, in natural modesty, hesitated to put to her, as they had only just met and she might find the proposition repugnant to her.

Her curiosity aroused, Ellen begged him to tell her the plan and not spare her feelings.

Mr. Grimsditch's plan, Edward explained, was that Ellen should marry him, and then his uncle, the Kendal banker, would make a handsome life settlement upon them which would include Shrigley—thus preventing her parents being turned out of their home and solving their desperate problem.

There was some dispute in the proceedings which later followed as to the terms in which Edward made his proposal and exactly when he made it and she accepted it.

Ellen said in her evidence at Lancaster the following year: "He said it had been suggested by Grimsditch that he should be my husband, then the property would be mine, and it would be in my power to turn papa out of doors if I liked, but, of course, I could not think of doing that."

After she had recovered from the astonishment of this proposal, she said to Edward: "I must see my Papa first."

So a deeper plot had to be hatched by the brothers. When they reached Carlisle they enacted another heartless little drama in order to bring the final pressure upon the reluctant girl.

Ellen now was expecting to meet her father at last. It was only reasonable—especially if she was to be married, and for such a reason, too. They would have to concoct a pretty good story to persuade her to marry Edward without seeing her father first.

Such ingenuity was not beyond Edward, and William loyally backed him up in the unscrupulous piece of play-acting which took place on their arrival at Carlisle.

They pulled up outside the Bush Hotel, and leaving Ellen once more in the carriage under the protection of Thévenot, the two brothers went into the hotel.

Ellen, of course, was noticed in the carriage, and evidence was given later about her downcast, even distressed appearance. This was not really surprising, considering she had been travelling for more than twenty-four hours without proper rest and had just been told that her father was ruined.

Presently the brothers returned.

Edward told her that they had seen her father and Grimsditch in a back room at the Bush. But her father was in hiding from the bailiffs who were after him to arrest him and throw him into prison for debt. He had made two vain attempts to cross the border into Scotland to escape them, but he could not now get out of the hotel undetected. If Ellen went in to see him, the bailiffs, who were among the crowd outside, would follow her in to where he was hiding and arrest him.

Edward said, Ellen later stated in court: " My Papa requested me if I ever loved him I would not hesitate to accept him as my husband. I was induced to consent by the fear that if I did not, my father would be ruined."

Later on, Wakefield, in his statement about what happened, said that he begged her not to say yes if she had any doubts about being happy with him. After all, some other way might be found of arranging her father's affairs—there was no absolute necessity for the marriage. But according to Wakefield, she said " yes—with pleasure for Papa's sake ". " She evidently exulted at the idea of being useful to her parents, and expressed so beautifully her admirable feeling towards them that I was very near clasping her in my arms and betraying all."

Why did Wakefield do it? What were his true motives? He had a reasonably good income for life. He was not in dire need of the Turners' money, unless he wanted some capital to settle upon his children. But if that was the reason, surely he would have gone about it differently, wooed the girl properly, and approached her father in a businesslike manner as he did over his first marriage. By the standards of the time, it was not such an incompatible match.

Edward's act was astonishing and incomprehensible. He could not have imagined that he would have got away with it. Could he seriously believe that she would ever forgive him for this cruel deception?

He explained his action later by saying that he had formed the impulsive design of boosting the new-rich Mr. Turner's prestige at Chester Assizes by marrying his daughter beforehand and bringing a troop of his fashionable friends to swell the incoming Sheriff's escort and mortify the county snobs. " The apparent impossibility of the thing urged me on."

This explanation, considered preposterous in some quarters in view of Wakefield's subsequent rise to fame and distinction, may be nearer the truth than any other.

In the 1820's, was he not a typical product of that shallow and vulgar world of fashion in which he moved in London, and to avoid which his better self made him retreat to the intellectual realities of Paris?

His less pleasant side showed itself in Turin in 1818 when at a fête given in honour of the Grand Duke Michael of Russia, Wakefield publicly insulted an English linen draper who arrived unsuitably dressed and who in Wakefield's opinion was rubbing shoulders too closely with his social superiors. The linen draper promptly challenged Wakefield, but Wakefield refused to duel with such a low-class person. The linen draper then returned the insult to Wakefield in public. Wakefield still avoided the duel, and the whole thing was finally smoothed over by the British Minister, with small credit for Wakefield.

He was undoubtedly a very arrogant young man. Those Regency dandies were the delinquents of their day. They were heartless, sneering, offensive, rude and overbearing to their social inferiors.

" Their motto," says Arthur Bryant in *The Age of Elegance*, " was to be ripe for any spree, by which they generally meant any frolic that involved others in trouble."

The dandy was a cad who sneered at everything and cared nothing for the feelings and sufferings of others. Violence and uproar, cruel jokes and pranks were their delight, and they had their imitators among all walks of society.

There is no suggestion that Edward Gibbon Wakefield was one of these Regency thugs, but undoubtedly he was infected by the spirit of vanity, uncharitableness and greed which characterised English society during the years just after Waterloo. In a society which worshipped money, the pursuit and carrying off of heiresses was a commonplace.

Was the abduction of Ellen Turner a wild jape that ended in disaster, or did Edward seriously think he could get away with it and get the girl and her money?

While he may have felt romantically inclined towards her during the time they were together, he never claimed to have been in love with her. If at the trial he had pleaded that his action was due to an unconquerable and irresistible passion for the girl, perhaps the story would have ended differently. But he made no such claim. He was fond of her all right. She grew on him. But that was all.

And then, having married her, why did he not have sexual intercourse with her?

This is a vital and interesting point. If the marriage had been consummated he would probably have got away with it. True, Ellen might not have forgiven the cruel deception by which he had won her, but the parents of a deflowered girl, perhaps with a child on the way, would almost certainly not in the 1820's have pressed charges against her abductor.

And so, having finally got the girl to agree, Wakefield ordered horses for Gretna.

The golden age of Gretna Green was between 1754 and 1856. Prior to 1754, runaway couples used to get married at the Fleet Prison, London, the ceremony being conducted by dishonest clergymen. This was stopped by Lord Hardwick's Marriage Act of 1754 by which all couples marrying in England had to publish banns. In 1856, a law was passed requiring one of the contracting parties of Scottish weddings to reside in Scotland three weeks previous to the marriage.

The Hardwick Act stopped the notorious Fleet marriages, but it did not apply to Scotland and the astute inhabitants of Gretna Green, which is nine miles north of Carlisle, just on the border, soon cashed in on the situation.

All the eloping couples had to do was to declare their wish to marry, in the presence of witnesses, and the ceremony was legal. It was usually performed by the blacksmith, but the tollkeeper, or the ferryman—in fact any person—might officiate. The 1820's were the great days of Gretna, and in one year as many as 200 couples were married at the tollhouse. There was no doubt that these marriages were perfectly legal.

The Gretna racket was parcelled out among various local families, some of whom became celebrities, and business was very good in the 1820's. There were pickings for all, and they had their scouts and agents at Carlisle, the last stage before Gretna, where their own postilions met the coaches of eloping couples and guided them to the appropriate establishment at Gretna.

Wakefield and Ellen went to David Laing, a well-known Gretna character who was later to cause something of a sensation at the Wakefield trial.

According to Edward, the drive from Carlisle to Gretna was made with himself and Ellen in high spirits, talking about the hair-raising escapes of other runaway couples, and imagining what her Cheshire friends would say when they knew what had happened.

At Gretna they both stood before old David Laing and he asked them the usual questions—their names, where they came from, whether they were free to marry, and whether they took each other for a lawful wedded wife and husband. They joined hands and having declared themselves to be husband and wife in the presence of the witnesses, they then became lawful spouses according to the law of Scotland.

Edward slipped a ring on Ellen's finger and they kissed each other. Edward paid Laing thirty pounds for marrying them and then they had dinner and champagne, the Laing establishment being well equipped to cater for their customers' needs in this respect.

And so Wakefield and his girl bride left Gretna and turned south.

How did he expect to extricate himself from the situation he was now in? He was not in the ordinary position of a man who had eloped with an heiress. He had to make his peace not only with the girl's parents, but with the girl herself. Her reaction when she found out how cruelly he had deceived her was fairly predictable.

And, of course, she would find out sooner or later. He couldn't conceal it from her for long.

There is reason to believe that Edward imagined that, given a little time, he could persuade her to accept the situation and forgive him, which seems to suggest that he knew little about girls.

They returned to Carlisle where the excited bride expected to throw herself into the grateful arms of her papa in the proud and happy knowledge that by marrying this near stranger she had saved the family fortune. But when they arrived at the Bush. Edward went inside the hotel and returned to say that her father had left hurriedly for London to settle his affairs.

And so they, too, left for London. Edward's plan was to take Ellen to Calais, then on to Paris, and stay in France, waiting to see what the Turner family reaction would be. He hoped that they would reconcile themselves to the *fait accompli*.

In the evening they arrived at Penrith and Edward booked separate rooms at the Crown Hotel.

It is probable that Ellen was innocent enough not to be surprised that her bridegroom did not share her bed with her. Brides of those days very often knew nothing at all about sex until the first rude encounter on their wedding night—a shock, of course, but most of them got over it. Ellen may well have expected nothing more intimate than an affectionate brother-and-sister relationship. That would have fulfilled her naïve ideas of romance. That was the only relationship that ever existed between her and Edward, and there is abundant evidence that she was radiantly happy all the time she was with him—until she found him out.

Why did Wakefield not sleep with his bride, as he was fully entitled to do, for they were legally married?

It was not that he thought her too young. A girl of fifteen was not considered too young in those days. This is a later conception, and it still lingers today. The magic age of sixteen was not legally established until the Offences Against the Person Act of 1861. Section 5 of the Criminal Law Amendment Act, 1885, made it a misdemeanour to have carnal knowledge of a girl under the age of sixteen, and the Age of Marriage Act, 1929, made void any marriage between two persons either of whom is under sixteen.

But in 1826 the Gretna marriage was legally binding, and Edward was fully entitled to his marital rights. But he did not take them.

He must have known that if he had had sexual intercourse with Ellen, his position in the event of difficulty with her family would have been much stronger. If he had consummated the marriage, he would probably have been spared the disaster of the trial and the horrors of Newgate.

It is not likely that a respectable middle-class family like the Turners would have upset the marriage if Ellen had lost her virginity, and possibly even been pregnant. They would undoubtedly have made the best of things, rather than have their only child, a tarnished, unmarried daughter, on their hands, and Wakefield would have got what he wanted in the end.

This hesitation to deprive Ellen of her virginity is interesting and is perhaps a vital clue to the mystery presented by such a man as Edward Gibbon Wakefield playing this unchivalrous trick upon an innocent girl.

The most likely explanation is that his conscience would not let him take and enjoy that which he had gained in such a shabby transaction. He could not go through with it.

He could have escaped to the world's end with his bride, but he determined instead, he said, to face it out with her family, and set the matter straight. Perhaps the appealing sweetness and delightful personality of the girl, to which he publicly attested, had shamed him into not taking the ultimate prize of her body without first facing up to what he had done—as much with her family as with her. The family, of course, was vitally important, seeing that the girl's fortune was at stake.

And so Ellen retained her priceless maidenhead, a treasure which was to cost Edward dear.

The following morning, Thursday—the third day of Ellen's remarkable adventure, the party set out from Penrith and travelled south.

At Leeds, William left them, going to Macclesfield to join Frances, and to find Ellen's father and tell him what had happened. William also was Paris-bound, and he and Emily Shelley-Sidney planned to marry there immediately.

William could not find Mr. Turner, so he left for Paris and was married to Emily a few days after his brother's Gretna marriage. They were desperately in love and the tragedy of their brief marriage is the saddest thing which was brought about by this rash and rather stupid act of abduction.

On the Friday of that week, Edward arrived in London with his virgin wife and they passed the night in two separate rooms at the Brunswick Hotel, Hanover Square.

The story was now out, and the account of the Gretna wedding was in the London papers the following day. Edward was warned by a friend that he had better be out of the country quickly, or he would be arrested, so the couple left for Dover on the Saturday morning, with Ellen still believing they were following her elusive father. They crossed the Channel the same day and put up at the Hotel Quillac at Calais.

In the meantime there was, of course, great alarm and consternation in the Turner family. Panic reigned in the Daulby establishment when they discovered that Ellen had not arrived at Shrigley and a weeping Miss Daulby informed Mr. Turner that his daughter had been abducted.

The Turner family instantly started the pursuit. They traced the runaways to Manchester, and thence to Huddersfield, but after that they lost the trail.

They did not think of riding post haste to Gretna, for they could not have foreseen the ingenious way in which Wakefield deceived the girl into going there with him.

It was on Tuesday morning that Ellen disappeared. By Wednesday she was wed to her abductor. On that day, Edward posted a letter in Carlisle to William Turner at Shrigley telling him he had married Ellen and begging that Mr. and Mrs. Turner " would render themselves quite easy " and that there was nothing for them to worry about, for their daughter was well and very happy.

This letter did nothing to calm or console William Turner. He was determined to put a stop to the marriage at all costs, and was not in any way content that his daughter, whom he loved dearly, should be treated in this way by a fashionable London fortune-hunter.

In the 1820's, the only effective police force in the country was in London, and Turner and his brother Robert and brother-in-law Robert Critchley instantly took horse to the metropolis to seek the aid of the Bow Street Runners.

The runaway couple's movements were soon traced, and when it was discovered that they were in Calais, Turner was able to obtain a letter from Canning, the Foreign Secretary, to Lord Granville, the British Ambassador in Paris, asking him to expedite the repatriation of the abducted girl, whose story was now in all the newspapers and the talk of London.

There were no extradition treaties in those days, and criminals were given up or not rather at the whim of the government of the country to which they had fled. It was possible that France, smarting under her defeat by the Allies in the Napoleonic Wars, might well have sheltered the fugitive Wakefield, despite Granville's efforts.

William Turner himself did not go to Calais. He sent the two Roberts (Ellen's uncles), Grimsditch the solicitor, and the police officer Ellis.

The rescue party were under instructions to be cautious. The separate rooms the couple had slept in at the Brunswick led the Turner family to hope that the marriage had not been consummated. If that was so, there was to be no mercy for Edward Gibbon Wakefield. If, however, Wakefield had claimed his nuptial rights by the time the uncles caught up with the pair, the Turner anger would have to be restrained in the girl's interests.

And so Edward's hesitation to consummate the marriage was fatal to his cause.

The rescue party had little difficulty in finding the fugitives and from all accounts the encounter was charged with true nineteenth-century drama.

Edward saw from the start that he could only fight a rearguard action. Ellen, who had been seen in Calais hanging on to his arm in the most affectionate manner, turned from him in revulsion when she heard the truth of what had happened.

" Oh, he is a brute !" she cried pathetically. " He has deceived me. And I never called anyone a brute before."

Wakefield appealed to the civic authorities, saying Ellen should not be taken from him by force. But when the Mayor observed that it was Uncle Robert's arm to which Ellen now clung for protection against the man who had betrayed her, His Worship saw that force would be required to keep the girl at her husband's side, and decided not to intervene.

Edward, seeing the whole game was up, told Uncle Robert to take Ellen home and, according to one report expressed himself in the following improbable terms: " Then, sir, you may dispose of your niece as you think proper, but you receive her at my hands as a pure and spotless virgin."

Robert Turner asked him if he would put this down in writing, and Edward wrote a declaration that no familiarities had passed between him and Ellen.

Having won the day completely, and received Ellen back in her virginal state, the Turner faction were not content to let it go at that. They wanted to take back Edward with them under arrest, and Ellis, the Bow Street Runner, had his handcuffs all ready.

But now the wretched Edward flatly refused to let Ellis take him in charge. The man had no authority anyway on French soil. He gave an undertaking that he would return to England to settle the affair after first going to Paris on his own business.

And so Ellen returned to the bosom of her family, deeply wounded and disillusioned at what Edward had done to her. She never forgave him.

Meanwhile, Edward was in Paris with his children and Phyllida Bathurst to console him. When he arrived the children were expecting him to bring Ellen with him and were making posies for their stepmother. It was not a happy homecoming.

And what of William? Having married Emily, he wanted to take her back to England. There was at first some difficulty with the British Embassy in Paris over the passport, the Ambassador being somewhat agitated by Canning's letter and the Turner abduction, which was being treated very seriously in England.

William had to swear an affidavit that he only wanted the passport to take his wife back to her family in England, and the
passport was granted.

When they disembarked at Dover, William was arrested, and
his weeping wife, who was never to see him again, was taken
from his arms for ever.

As soon as he got to Paris, Edward wrote to his brother:

My dear William—I write in haste to give you the news.
Mr. Robert Turner, Mr. Critchley and Grimsditch arrived by
the packet today with warrants etc. Ellen told all and was
anxious to leave me when she knew all. I expected as much
and therefore made a merit of necessity and let her go. They
tried to take me; but for that they were on the wrong side of
the water, as I well knew. I made and gave in writing a
solemn declaration that she and I had been as brother and
sister. How this will affect the validity of the marriage I know
not. I am now in a stew about you and wish that you were
safe. There can be no doubt that the law can punish us. For
myself I will meet it, come what may; but if you are able,
get away as soon as possible. The grand question now is: is
the marriage legal? They all said no and quoted William and
Mary upon me till I was tired of Their Majesties' names. Do
not stay. You can do no good. I shall go to England as soon
as possible. Upon this you may depend. Pray write but say
nothing to anybody. I am the person to speak—Yours,
Edward.

Edward returned to England in the middle of April 1826,
and gave himself up. Though he knew the law could punish
him, he knew also there would be some legal difficulties involved
in proceeding against him. In the absence of the Offences
Against the Person Act of 1861, the pinning of an offence upon
him proved a bit of a problem, especially as the authorities
would not have the Gretna marriage called into question. But
the problem was not beyond the ingenuity of the legal minds of
the time, and it is probable that the law was bent a little to en-
compass Wakefield's ruin.

He first appeared before a magistrate at Macclesfield, where a changed Ellen gave evidence against him, her pale expressionless face clearly telling him not to expect the slightest pity from her. She revenged herself upon him for his cruel deception by telling the court that she understood that the Gretna marriage certificate was only a kind of quittance which would save her father from ruin. She seemed to have forgotten the happiness of those few days they spent together and what it had meant to her.

She had, of course, been prompted what to say by Grimsditch, but in her bitterness and unhappiness she spoke the words willingly, which to Edward were like a blow across the face. The sad thing was that he had developed an affection for her, and he must have realised how richly he deserved the contempt which was implicit in her words.

The only thing that was said in Edward's favour was that he had been gentleman enough not to consummate the marriage; but this was probably said more as a public affirmation of Ellen's chastity than anything else.

Edward was committed for trial, but he had to spend eleven months incarcerated in Lancaster Castle before the trial took place.

The affair of the abduction in the meantime had become the object of intense public interest, and ribald pamphlets were published, asking how was it possible that Wakefield, having gone to all that elaborate trouble to get the girl, should not have slept with her? Among the reasons given for his refusal to enjoy the fruits of seduction were that he had venereal disease or was impotent.

The two brothers were tried at Lancaster in March 1827, before Baron Hullock. Frances Wakefield was also charged with her stepsons, as also was Edward's servant, Thévenot—though he remained discreetly in France and escaped justice.

The Wakefields were defended by James Scarlett, one of the great advocates of the day. His son, General Scarlett, later distinguished himself in the Crimean War commanding the successful Charge of the Heavy Brigade at Balaclava, which immediately preceded the disastrous Charge of the Light Brigade.

The indictment against the accused was in the following terms: that they "Not having any right or authority whatsoever did unlawfully take away and convey the said Ellen Turner out of the possession and against the will of the said Misses Daulby and for the sake of lucre and gain did conspire with divers other persons by false representations unlawfully to take and carry the said Ellen Turner being of the age of fifteen years and unlawfully cause the said Ellen Turner to contract matrimony with the said Edward Gibbon Wakefield unknowing of and to William Turner esquire, father of the said Ellen Turner who was then the only child and heir apparent unto William Turner, he then having substance, lands and tenements to the value of 5,000 l. by the year at Manchester."

This seems a curious indictment by modern standards but it was made to stand up in the law courts of the day, even though it does not appear to have been supported by an Act of Parliament.

The trial aroused great interest. Lancaster was packed with visitors, who came from far and wide to attend it.

Although it was pregnant with tragedy for the Wakefield brothers, there were elements of pantomime in the proceedings, particularly the evidence of old David Laing of Gretna Green, a picturesque character who got the better of many verbal exchanges with counsel.

Unfortunately, the old man caught a chill on his way home to Gretna and died.

One thing the prosecution could not do was to upset the legality of the Gretna wedding. That would have had too many repercussions, as a number of distinguished people had been married there. The Gretna wedding could only be upset by an Act of Parliament.

The prosecution had little difficulty in proving the abduction. Edward's callous deception of the girl who had put her trust in him could not be denied, and placed him in the worst possible light. The jury found them guilty without leaving the box and each brother was sentenced to three years' imprisonment; William to serve his at Lancaster Castle, Edward at Newgate. Frances had also been found guilty, but the Turners were not anxious to press the charge against her and she was not sentenced.

The Turners were determined to annul the marriage, and Lord Redesdale brought a Bill in the House of Lords to do this. Edward was taken from Newgate to attend the second reading. He claimed not to have been given sufficient notice to oppose the measure effectively, but his plea was overruled, and the measure was passed.

This was the last time Edward saw the girl with whom he had shared that strange adventure, and with whom he may possibly have been in love, for he never married again.

He went back to Newgate, thinking perhaps that life had ended for him.

Whatever Edward may have felt, for William tragedy was complete. The trial had utterly broken Emily's heart. Four months after it she died, and the following obituary notice appeared in *The Times*:

> DIED. On Sunday last at Quiddenham, the Seat of her uncle, the Earl of Albermarle, to the great affliction of her near relatives, and the sincere regret of numerous acquaintances, Mrs. William Wakefield. This accomplished and beautiful young lady has fallen a victim to a broken heart in consequence of the distant imprisonment of her youthful husband, who, in an inadvertent moment, joined his elder brother (Edward Gibbon Wakefield) in the mad prank of taking away a young lady to Gretna Green. Mrs. Wakefield was the only daughter of Sir John Sidney, Bart, of Penshurst Place in Kent, to which place her remains are to be removed, and great niece of Mr. Coke of Holkham. She left an infant daughter six months old.

Both Wakefield brothers lived down the disgrace of their " mad prank " and distinguished themselves in after life. Their later accomplishments brought them satisfaction and happiness.

But to the two girls whom they loved at the time when they blazed across the skies of scandal, they brought neither happiness nor long life.

Poor Ellen died almost as tragically as Emily. In 1829 she married a man named Legh, a person of both wealth and position in the north of England, but died in giving birth to her first child, another Ellen.

Judith Morton

JUDITH MORTON was one of those legendary creatures who hardly appeared in the close-printed newspaper columns of her day, but who was a true inspiration to murder—a nineteenth-century Lady Macbeth.

So far as I know she was never accused, or even officially suspected, of any crime. But at least two men were killed at her behest, and for the most elemental reason—because she had tired of one and wanted the other.

Her story was told with various embellishments by Victorian social workers until she became allegorical of what would happen to a man who got into the clutches of a wicked and designing Jezebel. Church missionaries in mid-century workhouses used her legend as a terrible example to men who go after unprincipled women.

In Westmorland, where she was born, and lived as a girl, the legend of her fatal beauty and charm, and the stories of the men who fought to possess her, were told till the end of the century; and there was a small clearing in Gilgraith Forest, not far from Appleby, where no one would dare to go after dark, for it was said to be the trysting place of Judith Morton and the two men who died because of her evil enchantment.

Near the village pump at Bedstone there was a pond in which an old woman was drowned as a witch in the year after Waterloo. Judith, then a little girl, had been the only child who had dared to go near the ducking-stool, and it was said the witch cast her eye on young Judith and cursed her before she died.

Judith finished her life in the United States, and her legend followed her there to Philadelphia where the owner of a large store fell hopelessly under her spell and killed for her.

There are various stories about her end. It was said that from Philadelphia she went to the deep South where she married a plantation owner and was eventually killed by a negro slave. Another story was that well after the Civil War she was in San Francisco running a gambling saloon which became notorious for shootings.

Judith, of course, was wickedly provocative and in many ways callous, but she may not have been as evil as the mid-century moralists made out. The only certain story about her was that told by perhaps her principal victim, Richard Penson, who recounted it to a church missionary in a midlands workhouse not long before he died.

Richard Penson's father was a " statesman "—which in the north of England means a small landowner who farms his own estate. Judith Morton's father was a landowner of some means. Both families farmed not very far from Appleby. But whereas the Mortons prospered, the fortunes of the Pensons continually declined.

Judith was more than just the local beauty. She was the most sought-after girl in Westmorland. Her beaux included Charles Harpur, son of a landowner, Robert Masters, whose family bred horses on the slopes of the fells, and Richard Penson. She had other admirers. But these three are the ones that concern this strange story.

Judith had given Richard Penson very good reason to think that he was the favoured suitor. He did not take his two rivals very seriously. He knew them both well. He liked Harpur, though he could not stand Masters, whom he considered smug, supercilious and self-satisfied.

Richard's mother had died some years previously, and he was an only child. While his father lived, the fact that the family estate was practically insolvent was obvious to no one. Up until Penson senior's death, father and son lived in comfortable circumstances, and Richard now looked as though he might retrieve the family fortunes by marrying the Morton girl, herself an only child and something of an heiress.

Mr. Penson died suddenly, leaving his son barely £200 after his debts had been settled. Richard's only other assets were a good appearance and education, and he had reason to believe that, despite his slender fortune, he could marry the girl he loved.

The fact that she was better off than he was did not really weigh with Richard. He was genuinely in love with Judith. He knew she was a proud and independent girl, who was known to do daring and unusual things. But Richard, in his innocence of women and the world, passionately believed she was the girl for him, and would be a wife of whom he could be proud.

He sadly misjudged his chances with the exciting and desirable Judith, now just seventeen, in the youthful bloom of her startling beauty.

She rejected his proposal with scorn. Did he really imagine she would marry the son of a poverty-stricken farmer who had barely a few pennies to rub together? She told him bluntly that the man she married would have to have position.

The heartbroken Richard at first considered doing away with himself. But he rejected this course and took the sensible view that he would accept her challenge and go to London to seek both fortune and position. Then she would have to take his proposal seriously.

Selling up in Westmorland, he went to London and became articled to a solicitor with offices near the Old Bailey, who, in exchange for the bulk of Richard's £200, taught him law and gave him a small salary. The solicitor soon saw that young Penson had the makings of a good lawyer with a clever turn of mind. He worked hard and studied long hours and, after serving his agreed term of five years, he passed his examinations and was admitted to the Court of King's Bench as an attorney.

Having gained at least position, if not fortune, Richard now returned to Westmorland to press once more his suit with the girl he adored, and whom he had not forgotten for a moment during those long five years. He had written to her, but her

146

replies had been desultory and not very informative. He was not discouraged by that, believing that Judith, like many people, was not a good letter-writer. He had not at any time been untrue to her. But he did not imagine that she had ceased to amuse herself with her many admirers. He did not believe that she took any of them seriously.

She was now twenty-two and more beautiful than ever. Her father had died a few months previously, leaving her a small but comfortable fortune. Judith was now her own mistress, full of self-confidence and very conscious of her power over the opposite sex.

She received Richard with more graciousness than she had done at their last meeting. They had both grown up. He had lost the look of the country born-and-bred youth, and there was something of the sophisticated stamp of Regency London about him. All the same he was soon to learn, with more delicacy this time, that it was still useless to hope that this imperious young lady would bestow her affections upon him. She was in love with someone else.

His successful rival was Robert Masters, that long-standing admirer of hers whom Richard had known since youth, and never liked very much. He did not think Masters was worthy of her, and he told her so.

Judith thanked him for the compliment, smiled mysteriously and said no more.

Heartbroken again, Richard left the Morton estate in the shadow of the fells and rode south, first to Appleby, where there seemed to be no opening for him, then to Liverpool, where he opened a solicitor's office in Scotland Road.

Liverpool was in the middle of a slump. The port had flourished for a hundred years on the slave trade. At the end of the century, five-sixths of the world's trade in human flesh had been centred in Liverpool. The trade was abolished by law in 1807 and prosperity in the Mersey died until the coming of steam.

Richard arrived there at the wrong time. There was little employment for any young solicitor and he decided to return to London and try and get work with the firm in Old Bailey to which he had been articled.

147

But suddenly fate stepped in unexpectedly and dramatically to alter his whole life.

Robert Masters, his successful rival for Judith, was murdered. The Westmorland county papers were full of it. That other admirer of hers, Charles Harpur, was involved, and Judith herself was the centre of the triangle.

Charles had been to America, where he had done well, and had returned home on a visit. As with Richard, he immediately returned to his old love—this girl who haunted them and whom they could never forget.

Robert Masters, to whom she was now apparently betrothed, was instantly jealous. The two men met at a farmers' dinner and quarrelled over her. They came to blows and had to be parted by the other guests.

A few days later, Masters' body was found in a small clearing in Gilgraith Forest, shot through the heart. His gold watch and money were missing.

At first it seemed that the motive was obvious and that all the authorities had to do was to catch the tramp or highwayman responsible.

Then a man named James Blundell went to the authorities with a story that placed a very different complexion on the affair. Blundell was a small farmer—a " statesman "—of some repute and his story could not be discounted.

He said that on the night before Masters' body was found in the clearing, he was returning home along an isolated path on the outskirts of Gilgraith Forest, when he heard a pistol shot.

Barely a minute later, while Blundell was trying to make out what was happening, a young man ran through the trees from the direction of the clearing, pistol in hand. He stood for a second in the lane, fully revealed in the bright moonlight as Charles Harpur, whom Blundell knew, then plunged into the bushes on the other side of the pathway and vanished.

Harpur was immediately arrested and charged with the murder.

Richard was considerably disturbed by the affair, knowing as he did the three people whom it so closely concerned. He debated with himself whether to go to Gilgraith and find out more about the affair—and perhaps be of some assistance to Charles Harpur, whom he had always liked, despite the fact that they were rivals for Judith. Who could blame him for committing a crime for her? Who wouldn't? But murder . . . Perhaps it wasn't murder, but manslaughter. There must have been some kind of fight. Masters was insanely jealous of Judith now, and he had already provoked Charles to blows at the farmers' dinner. Richard couldn't imagine Charles murdering anyone—certainly not in cold blood.

He was debating thus with himself when he heard the clatter of hooves, the jingle of harness and the sound of carriage wheels drawing up outside his unpretentious office. He went quickly to the window, and saw, to his surprise and excitement, Judith Morton step from the carriage.

Richard hurried to the street door to let her in. She swept into his little office in her elegant dark cloak, allowing his eager lips to brush her gloved hand for the barest moment.

He saw at once that she was disturbed and upset, as indeed she had good cause to be. The dark clothes she wore under her travelling cloak were evidence of the sorrow she must have felt at the tragic death of her betrothed. At least that was what Richard thought.

But with all her distress, she was the same Judith, with her dark magnetic eyes, her inviting mouth, the animal grace of her movements. Was there ever a more exciting and desirable woman? Richard asked himself. In all London he had not seen a woman who had so much of what we now call sex appeal.

He instantly offered his condolences for the tragedy which had encompassed her.

She dabbed a damp eye with a tiny lace handkerchief. " Poor Robert—poor Charles. But this thing is more terrible, more far-reaching than you think."

When he asked for an explanation of her words, she did not offer one immediately. She told him that she had come to consult him professionally and first of all offered him a fifty-pound Bank of England note to secure his services. Despite his assurance that it was quite unnecessary to pay him such a large sum before he had done anything for her, she insisted, knowing full well his financial position, and he finally accepted the note.

She then produced from her reticule a packet which she told him contained copies of depositions made in connection with the murder charge against Charles Harpur. She asked him to read them and give her his professional opinion on the case.

It did not take him long to read them while she sat there anxiously, her dark eyes on him all the time. There could be only one opinion on the depositions. They constituted a *prima facie* case against Harpur.

" There can be little doubt that he killed Bob Masters," said Richard. " I don't know what Charles' defence is. Possibly the charge could be reduced to manslaughter."

" What about the missing watch and money?" she asked.

" The police obviously believe Charles Harpur took them in order to cause confusion. The prosecution won't have much difficulty in persuading a jury of that, either."

" What about Blundell?" she asked. " Didn't you know he owed Robert a lot of money?"

Richard did know, but did not see how that could help Harpur's defence. It was well known that Charles Harpur and Robert Masters were quarrelling bitterly over Judith.

They discussed the details of the case for a while, and then Judith let off her bombshell. She had no need to bind Richard to secrecy. He was utterly her slave. He was ready body and soul at her service.

" I killed Robert," she said. " That is what I have really come to tell you."

After she had convinced him that this was not some mad joke, she told him the story.

A week after Richard's visit to her when she told him of her betrothal to Masters, Charles Harpur arrived home from America. She had always been in love with him and had preferred him to Robert Masters, so she broke off her engagement to Robert and became engaged to Charles. This infuriated Robert, who told her that if she did not give Charles up, he would show Charles all the letters she had written to him.

Some of these letters, she explained, were written when she was nineteen and were a little indiscreet. She certainly did not want Charles, who had rather old-fashioned ideas, to see them.

" He is also hot-headed and jealous," she continued, " as I am sure you know, Richard, and I was afraid of what he might do—either to me or Robert—if he saw the letters. So, in an awful state of mind, I wrote to Robert demanding in the name of his honour and his manliness that he should return the letters to me."

Robert, she said, seemed affected by her appeal, and promised that if she met him at nine o'clock on a certain evening in the little clearing in Gilgraith Forest, their old trysting place, he would return the letters—if he could not persuade her to break it off with Charles.

She agreed, prepared to risk an acrimonious scene with her discarded lover in order to get her letters back. She took her father's pistols with her as she was riding alone at night and there had been a number of tramps and footpads recently in the lonely Gilgraith Forest.

She met Robert as arranged in the clearing. He instantly started to argue with her, trying to persuade her to give up Charles and renew her engagement to him. She was firm in her refusal, and equally firm in her insistence that he should keep his promise and return the letters to her.

He mocked her, taking one of the letters from his pocket, reading from it one of the more burning love passages she had written to him three years previously.

Judith said that she now lost her temper and made a snatch for the letter. There was a struggle. Her hand quite involuntarily closed on one of the pistols. There was a flash and a report and Robert suddenly dropped dead at her feet.

" What followed," she said in a voice that nearly broke, " I can only confusedly describe. For some minutes I was too distracted to do anything but stare at Robert. With the white light from the moon on his face and his teeth showing in a kind of grin, he looked awful, Richard."

Richard, listening to her story, was as shocked as she was. Though he was bitter with jealousy himself, he was full of sympathy for her, and realised that it was he she had now turned to, and that was something of a consolation.

When she had recovered from the shock, she continued, she suddenly became cunning and went through Robert's pockets. She took not only all her letters, but also his watch and money to make it look as though he had been killed by a footpad.

She heard someone approaching and became really terrified, until it turned out to be Charles Harpur. He had called at her house and, hearing the direction she had taken, had followed her to the clearing in Gilgraith Forest, knowing the place well, having often had romantic meetings with her there—as indeed Richard had in the years past.

"Knowing I could trust Charles with my life," she said, " I told him everything and he has kept silent, even though he now lies under the shadow of the scaffold."

What was she to do?

Richard believed her story, but did not think that a judge and jury would. His advice was that she should say nothing and that he too would keep silent.

What—save herself at the expense of the innocent Charles' life! Judith would not hear of it. She would rather give herself up and throw herself on the mercy of the courts.

She begged Richard to think of a way of saving both of them. She had heard that he was an astute lawyer.

It would take more than mere astuteness to save Judith and her lover, as Richard well knew.

"Do you still love me, Richard?" she asked.

He had to admit his hopeless infatuation which had grown stronger with the years of longing. The story of violence she had just told him, the fickleness and indiscretions she had just admitted, made no difference to his blind adoration. He was utterly consumed by her, completely in her power.

She now told him that she could never marry Charles after what had happened, and that although Charles would rather die on the scaffold than betray her secret, he now felt differently towards her. He would never care for her again, as he once did. If Richard proved his devotion to her by saving them both, then, who knows, she might reward him by giving him his greatest desire.

Buoyed up by a tremendous hope, Richard then threw every

ounce of his energy into the formidable problem of putting up a defence which would gain Charles Harpur an acquittal without incriminating Judith in any way.

The truth would certainly acquit Charles, but equally as certainly give Judith a long term of imprisonment. Even if her story that Masters' death was accidental was believed, the attempt to deceive the law would count heavily against her. She might even be found guilty of deliberate murder and hanged.

The task then was to save Charles, prove him innocent. As Judith promptly suggested, the way to do that was to discredit the vital witness, Blundell.

Richard sat up half the night working out his plan. When he saw Judith the following day, he told her that the only way of saving Charles without implicating her would involve a considerable risk. It could be done, but they might have to flee the country afterwards.

Judith gave him to understand that, if they had to flee, they would go together, and Richard, thinking that he was about to gain what he wanted most in the whole world, set about laying his plans.

" Give me Masters' watch," he said. " I want to advertise a description of it. Then I must go and see Charles and tell him that we have a plan which will bring him an acquittal. Whatever happens, he must say nothing."

" Tell him nothing of our plan either," urged Judith. " It would be best."

Richard agreed and immediately set to work on his plan for Harpur's defence, confident that his reward for his betrayal of all legal ethics would be the possession of the girl he desired almost more than life itself. Judith certainly encouraged him to believe that this would be so.

Charles Harpur's trial took place at Appleby Assizes to a packed court. The prisoner's counsel, under instructions from Richard, rose to cross-examine only one of the prosecution's witnesses—James Blundell, upon the truth of whose evidence the Crown's case almost entirely rested.

It was immediately obvious that the defence's tactics were to throw suspicion for the murder upon Blundell, who admittedly was on the spot at the time of the shooting. Great play was made of the fact that Blundell owed money to the murdered man, and Blundell had to admit that Masters had threatened to foreclose on his farm if he did not pay up.

Blundell was treated with great harshness in the box, and he did not make a good witness. A raw countryman, unused to the ways of the world outside the fells, he was easily confused and made to say things which were practically self-incriminatory —so much so that when he left the witness box he was instructed to remain within the precincts of the court.

The defence then opened its case and Richard brought on only one witness—a very respectable-looking middle-aged gentleman by the name of Thomas Aldous.

Aldous said he owned a large pawnbroking establishment in Blackfriars Road, Southwark, and that he had answered an advertisement put in the London papers by Mr. Richard Penson, the prisoner's solicitor, concerning a gold watch. This gold watch he produced in court. He declared that it had been pledged with his firm a short while after the date of the murder by a man who gave his name as Frederick Smith and his address as 8 Lambeth Walk. He had since discovered that no such person lived at this address.

It remained only for the watch to be shown to John Masters, brother of the murdered man, who immediately identified it as that worn by his brother Robert on the night of his death.

The benign and respectable Mr. Aldous then merely had to identify James Blundell as the man who had pawned the murdered man's watch, and Richard's clever little trick upon justice worked completely. Charles Harpur was immediately acquitted and Blundell, shouting his innocence with such passion that he almost collapsed with apoplexy, was arrested.

Richard was well aware that his trick would soon be discovered, and arrangements for instant flight had already been made. In those days justice moved slowly, and pursuit abroad and extradition was not always possible.

In the case of Ellen Turner (q.v.) the fugitives were pursued by relatives and a privately engaged Bow Street Runner, but they had no power to arrest the culprit in France and the French government almost certainly would not have extradited him.

While fugitives in those days could usually find some haven of safety somewhere in Europe, the safest place of all was always America—known then as the land of liberty. The United States had gained independence from the yoke of colonialism only recently, and her relations with the ex-mother country—with the notorious George III hardly cold in his grave—were wary and suspicious. All fugitives were welcome in the great nation which was building up in the New World. Richard knew he had only to get there with Judith to be safe.

Richard's first duty when the court broke up in great excitement at the dramatic turn of events was to pay off his false witness, whose name, of course, was not Aldous, and to tell him to get out of the district as soon as possible.

Richard had an appointment to see Judith after the trial, but at the hotel where they had arranged to meet, he found, instead of her, a note in her hand.

Thanks a million times for what you have done. I am confident that with your astuteness you will see that no harm comes to poor B. I will write to you in a few days—J.

He waited uneasily and impatiently, knowing that time was running short, and that before long the law would be after him for conspiring to perpetrate a perjury—a very serious offence. Harpur had vanished, and there was no sign of Judith. He went to the Morton estate on the borders of Gilgraith Forest. She was not there. The place was up for sale.

James Blundell quickly gathered his scattered senses and engaged a firm of Liverpool solicitors to look after his interests. They soon established not only that Blundell on the day when Aldous said he was in London pawning the watch, was indisputably in his home near Bedstone; but also that there was no such person as Thomas Aldous owning a pawnbroker's in Blackfriars Road.

Blundell's solicitors, realising that there had been a conspiracy against their client with the object of defeating justice, immediately informed the authorities, who issued warrants for the arrest of Richard Penson and Charles Harpur.

Richard had, however, booked passages for himself and Judith on a ship sailing from Liverpool to Boston a few days after the trial ended. This ship was now on the high seas and there was no means of communicating with it, or pursuing it. It was assumed that Richard and Judith were on board together. Once they reached America there would be no way of getting them back to face justice, so the case against Richard was dropped. There was no trace of Harpur either, and it was assumed that he, too, had fled to America, where he had been living before his visit to Westmorland which provoked the murder in Gilgraith Forest.

The murder was accordingly consigned to the list of unsolved crimes.

As for Richard Penson, he fled south to London, in constant fear of discovery and arrest, and completely crushed by the treacherous way Judith had forsaken him.

Though he changed his name, he remained in contact with a trusted friend in Liverpool who about a year later forwarded him the following letter from America:

> You were a poor fool, Richard. My husband and I are now safe and sound in the land of liberty, far beyond all possibility of pursuit. Charles is my second husband. I was married to him the day after Robert Masters, my first husband, was killed—Judith.

Judith did not confide to him what had really happened that night in Gilgraith Forest. But obviously it was not her hand that held the pistol. Could Richard ever have thought that it was? Blundell had no reason to lie when he said that Harpur came away from the scene of the shooting, gun in hand.

But Judith must have been there, too, when her husband was shot by Harpur, otherwise how would she have come by the watch? Did the two men quarrel over her as they had done previously, only in her presence this time? Judith enjoyed watching her men fight to the death over her. Such a scene was to be enacted again.

Clever lawyer he might have been, Richard Penson allowed himself to be utterly deceived by this woman. He should not have believed the story she told him. Perhaps he never did. He was just a willing, eager victim. Poor fool he certainly was. Could she have had anything but contempt for him?

Once on the downward path, he just slipped farther and farther down. Drink, women, petty crime—he became engulfed in the sleazy half-life of nineteenth-century London.

He developed consumption and ended up in the infirmary of a London workhouse where he told his story to a church missionary.

In his possession was a letter from one of his old friends in Westmorland enclosing a cutting from an American newspaper which was headed " Quick Work " and which read:

Three weeks ago, Mr. Charles Harpur, of Westmorland, England, thinking his friend, Mr. William Harrison, a storekeeper, of Philadelphia, was seeing too much of his young and beautiful wife, *née* Miss Judith Morton, also of Westmorland, England, challenged him to a duel. The encounter took place at midnight in a wood and proved fatal to Mr. Harpur. Mrs. Harpur, who was present during the encounter, at once became engaged to Mr. Harrison, and was married to him on Friday, exactly 18 days after her husband's death.

Charlotte Bryant

(1936)

THE TWO Charlottes in this book were both executed.

Charlotte Bryant was a thirty-three-year-old illiterate Irish nymphomaniac who was not at all to be compared with the glamorous Corday. They both paid the supreme penalty.

The Corday execution was not by the standards of the time an act of injustice. But this cannot be said with certainty about the hanging of Charlotte Bryant, on 15th July 1936, at Exeter Prison. Her case is yet another which arouses certain doubts about English justice.

The doubts in this case have been raised by an eminent Q.C., Mr. J. D. Casswell, who has seriously criticised the conduct of the Court of Criminal Appeal and the then Home Secretary, Sir John Simon.

Charlotte Bryant was a very immoral woman, and the suspicion cannot be resisted that her immorality counted against her, as it probably did with Edith Thompson and Ruth Ellis, and as it certainly did in some of those sultry Victorian trials. The puritan tradition dies hard.

Writing about Charlotte Bryant's case in 1961, " with special uneasiness ", Mr. Casswell says: " I am still, even after all this time, not convinced that her guilt was adequately or properly proved."*

What exactly does Mr. Casswell mean by this? That she was

---

* *A Lance For Liberty*, by J. D. Casswell, Q.C. (Harrap, 1961)

not guilty, or merely that her guilt was not proved? Two very different things.

But whatever he means, criticism from such a quarter is a serious thing. Unease about the justice meted out to people who have been hanged in recent years is disturbingly widespread. Timothy Evans is a classic case. Such suspected miscarriages of justice are powerful arguments for the abolitionists. Perhaps the most powerful argument; for the concept of the sacredness of human life is slightly ironic in the atomic age.

It is bad enough for a person to be wrongly punished for a crime. In the peculiar manner of English legal procedure, which can, and often does, disallow vital evidence (as in the A6 case), miscarriages of justice are more frequent than many people would care to admit. In cases where the punishment is imprisonment some restitution to a wrongly convicted person is possible. But no restitution is possible to the dead. There can be no question of bringing back the death penalty until certain aspects of English legal procedure are reformed.

The law being an ass is an English conception. Dickens was the first to say it, and it has been readily adopted as a truism. Neither the continentals nor the Americans hold their legal procedure in such contempt.

Charlotte Bryant, whether or not she was a martyr to English justice, had none of the qualities of a heroine. In fact she appeared to have no qualities at all. She certainly arouses our pity, for at the end she was infinitely pathetic.

She had neither looks nor charm. This Irish gipsy woman from Londonderry met Frederick Bryant, a farm labourer from Dorset, while he was serving with the Army in Ulster. They married, and after his discharge they lived in Dorset.

Bryant returned to his old job as cowman. Farm labouring in the depressed 'thirties was extremely ill-paid, and the Bryants found it difficult to make ends meet and to feed their growing family of children.

Charlotte undoubtedly had a very strong sex urge, and she soon acquired a certain reputation in the countryside around Yeovil where she frequented public houses, and for the price of a drink would go outside with any man for a quick roll in the hay. Sex, of course, paid even larger dividends than just the odd drink, and she was soon able to supplement her husband's meagre £1 18s. a week from the proceeds of her extra-marital activities.

She often brought her clients to her cottage at Coombe, a village near Sherborne, and would send her children out to buy sweets while she entertained her visitor.

Her husband knew what was going on all right, and as times were hard he tolerated it. Cream cakes and salmon were added to the family's diet and sometimes they hired a car for a holiday.

After a while Charlotte met a man named Leonard Parsons, a wandering salesman, who sometimes called himself Bill Moss. Parsons completely bowled her over. She fell madly in love with him.

Parsons did not create the impression of being a woman-killer, but there is no accounting for what attracts men and women together. Parsons was described by one of his previous mistresses as " a fancy woman's man—a man who would break up any home ".

This amorous wandering salesman, however, did not break up the Bryants' home. He just moved in as a lodger and slept with the wife. The cuckolded Bryant put up with this also, and was well aware of the fact that his wife's youngest child had been fathered by the lodger.

Bryant must have been a peculiar man. This kind of *ménage à trois* is perhaps not so rare as might be supposed; but as a rule the complaisant husband has something to gain from the situation he tolerates.

But it is difficult to see what Bryant had to gain, if one discounts the improbable reason that he was too much in love with his wife to leave her. Bryant was earning a miserable wage and was having to support a wife and five children—though undoubtedly Parsons contributed to the upkeep of the home as well.

Mrs. Bryant said later that it was for the sake of the children that the home was kept together, and this too may have been the reason for Bryant staying.

Parsons lived in the Bryants' home for two years, on and off, sharing wife as well as board with Bryant. Every now and then he left to resume his wandering life as a pedlar and to visit his " natural wife ", a gipsy, Priscilla Loveridge, and their four children, and Charlotte would go after him to persuade him to return to her. When Parsons was at the Bryants' cottage, the lady of the house gave herself to him with more than her usual abandon, neglecting even more her none-too-clean home.

Finally, in November 1935, Parsons decided to make the break for good. Charlotte was desolate, doing everything she knew to try and make him stay. She even told him that she expected to be a widow soon, and would he marry her then? According to his evidence, he told her that he would not.

This was all brought out later as evidence against her. She was desperate, they said, to keep her lover, even prepared to get rid of her husband so that she could marry him.

It is certainly true that after Parsons finally left the Bryants' home, Charlotte was very upset and scoured the countryside in vain looking for him. On 19th December she went to a gipsy encampment near Weston-super-Mare looking for him, and there she had an acrimonious encounter with Priscilla Loveridge.

But she did not find Parsons there. The next time she saw him was when he appeared in the witness box at her trial to give evidence against her. This must have been the bitterest moment of all for Charlotte, if she really did kill her husband in the hope that Parsons would marry her.

This theory would make more sense were it not for the appearance of another person in her life in 1935. This was a widow named Lucy Malvina Ostler, who had seven young children.

The two women met during the summer of that year and became great friends. After Leonard Parsons left in November, Mrs. Ostler suggested to Charlotte that they should all share the same house, so that the two women could baby-sit for each other.

Bryant was the only one who objected to this arrangement. He was prepared to put up with his wife sleeping with the lodger, but Mrs. Ostler's brood of seven was too much for him. He put his foot down. But to no avail. The Ostlers moved in.

According to the defence it was this situation which set off the train of events which led to Bryant's death, not Mrs. Bryant's compulsive passion for Parsons.

After all, her husband tolerated her prolonged affair with Parsons, and Parsons had told her he was not going to marry her. So what motive did she have for murdering her husband?

It is certainly conceivable that Charlotte had developed a contemptuous dislike for her admittedly despicable husband, and might have thought she would be better off without him and could support herself with her whoring. But did she seriously think she could whore with twelve small children in the cottage, even if Mrs. Ostler did baby-sit for her?

And even if she thought her husband's death would bring back Parsons to her, did she imagine the man would return to the cottage now that Mrs. Ostler and her brood were there?

If we accept Charlotte Bryant's guilt, the motive is far from clear.

Towards the end of 1935, Frederick Bryant had several attacks which the doctor diagnosed as gastro-enteritis. The doctor did not look for arsenical poisoning, the symptoms of which are similar.

A few days before Christmas, Bryant developed his last fatal attack. On the night of 21–22 December, he slept with Mrs. Bryant and their youngest child in the double bed. Sleeping on a chair in the same cramped bedroom was Mrs. Ostler.

According to Mrs. Ostler she woke up about three o'clock and heard Charlotte trying to get her husband to drink some Oxo. A few minutes later she heard sounds of him vomiting.

Mrs. Bryant, however, told a different story. She said she was " fagged out " and slept heavily all night. She did not even stir, and certainly gave her husband no Oxo. In the morning Mrs. Ostler said that Bryant had asked for water several times during the night and she had attended to him.

Anyway the following morning, 22nd December, Bryant was

taken to Sherborne Hospital where he died in the afternoon. Four grains of arsenic were found in his body.

The police instantly descended upon the cottage, while Charlotte and her children went to the "workhouse" at Sturminster. The police found a battered empty tin in a pile of garbage at the back of the cottage. Traces of arsenic were discovered in the tin which was identified by a firm which made weedkiller as one of their containers.

A Yeovil chemist reported that he had recently sold a tin of this weedkiller to a woman. As it contained arsenic he asked her to sign the poison register. But she could neither read nor write so she made a cross.

Both Charlotte Bryant and Mrs. Ostler were illiterate, and the police were fairly satisfied that one or other of them was guilty of administering the arsenic to the dead man. They were both arrested.

Protesting violently, they took part in an identification parade, but the chemist failed to pick either of them out.

This put the police in a difficult position. The identification of the person who bought the weedkiller was essential if they were to press their case. They continued to question the two women.

Then quite unexpectedly Lucy Ostler turned against her friend and volunteered a statement so damaging that it resulted in Charotte being immediately charged with murder.

Mrs. Ostler said that, just after Frederick Bryant's death, Charlotte had pointed to a green tin in a cupboard and said that she must get rid of it. Mrs. Ostler's description of the tin coincided in every detail with the tin of weedkiller sold by the Yeovil chemist. She also said that a few days later when raking the ashes under the Bryants' boiler she had found a burnt tin of the same size, which she threw on to the garbage pile.

Charlotte Bryant was charged on 10 February 1936, and she said, " I never got poison from anywhere and that people know. I don't see how they can say that I poisoned my husband."

The Crown set to work to build up its case against her. The late Dr. Gerald Roche Lynch, Senior Official Analyst to the Home Office, found arsenic in dust samples taken from the bed-

163

room where Bryant died and also a burnt tin found in the yard. This tin, however, was never properly identified as the one which Mrs. Ostler said she had found in the boiler ashes.

But Dr. Roche Lynch, after analysing the ashes in the boiler, found that they contained 149 parts to the million of arsenic. This he claimed was an abnormally high proportion, and from this expert opinion arises one of the big controversies of the case.

Dr. Lynch's findings were a strong corroboration of Mrs. Ostler's story of Charlotte's intention of getting rid of the weed-killer tin by burning it in the boiler, and so the case went before Mr. Justice MacKinnon at Dorchester Assizes on 27th May 1936, with the Crown confident it had an unanswerable case, although the Solicitor General (Sir Terence O'Connor, K.C.) admitted he was in no position " to give a convincing demonstration as to how death was brought about ".

Mrs. Ostler was the Crown's prime witness. People who knew her in the neighbourhood hardly recognised the sober, neatly dressed figure in the witness box giving evidence which was to put the rope around the neck of her best friend who sat a few yards away in the dock staring emptily at her.

Lucy Ostler said that, after the death of Bryant, Charlotte asked her what an inquest was. " I told her I thought it was a kind of operation and that if she could neither read nor write, nothing could be found. She said, ' If they can't find anything, they can't put a rope round me '." Mrs. Ostler said that Charlotte told her she hated her husband, but did not want to leave him, because of the children.

When Mr. J. D. Casswell cross-examined Mrs. Ostler, he caused a sensation by suggesting that she had been under suspicion in connection with the death of her own husband. She denied that she was frightened because the police suspected her and that was the reason she invented the whole story.

Later in the trial, Mr. Casswell withdrew a suggestion that there had been digging at the grave of Mrs. Ostler's husband, and the solicitor who instructed him was strongly criticised in the witness box by the Attorney General.

The defence's attempt to throw suspicion for the murder on

Lucy Ostler came to nothing. There was certainly no evidence against her.

All that could be extracted from her in cross-examination was the admission that she was frightened at having been put on the identification parade with Mrs. Bryant, though she denied that this had made her invent her statement implicating Charlotte. She admitted she was in the cottage during Bryant's illness, had helped to nurse him and give him his medicine and that she had had equal opportunity with Mrs. Bryant of giving him the arsenic. But she denied she wanted to share the cottage with the Bryants, or that Bryant objected to her and her children being there.

Parsons also gave evidence against Charlotte. Unkempt and unshaven, it was difficult to imagine him arousing female passion, and he seemed totally unaffected by Charlotte's fate. He had some difficulty in understanding such polite terminology as " intimate with ", but he admitted persistent adultery with Charlotte over a period of two years. He said she told him she was expecting to become a widow; but he had told her that he wouldn't marry her even if she was free. He denied the defence's suggestion that he had suggested to Mrs. Bryant that she should poison her husband.

A colourful appearance in court was made by the gipsy, Priscilla Loveridge, and her aged, pipe-smoking mother, an acrimonious old lady wearing a trilby hat and full of violent oaths against the accused. It was Priscilla Loveridge's opinion that Parsons was a woman's fancy man and a home-breaker. And who can say her nay? He may very well have been, despite his appearance. He certainly had Charlotte Bryant by the ears and she was a woman of vast sexual experience.

Charlotte went into the witness box on the third day of the trial and surprised her own counsel by proving a good witness whom the Attorney General was unable to shake. She strongly denied administering arsenic to her husband.

Her great bitterness against the man who betrayed her is understandable. " I do not like the man. I do not want him. Parsons was after me, not me after Parsons."

Dr. Roche Lynch's expert opinion that 149 parts to the million of arsenic in the fire ashes was abnormally high was an important part of the Crown's case and was mentioned by the judge in his summing-up.

The jury were an hour finding Charlotte guilty, and as the judge pronounced the sentence of death his voice faltered.

Perhaps it was not until that moment that Charlotte fully realised what was happening and what they were going to do to her, for she suddenly broke down. Her head went forward. She moaned and sobbed. She had to be half carried out of the dock in a state of collapse and down to the cells where she was attended by a doctor.

Mr. F. T. Giles, in his book *The Criminal Law*, says rather callously that a man, having just been sentenced to death " finds the condemned cell placed at his disposal with two warders constantly in attendance until the three Sundays thoughtfully provided by authority to allow him time to prepare himself for eternity, have elapsed."

Charlotte Bryant, however, had twice as long to " prepare herself for eternity ". She was sentenced at the end of May but was not hanged until the middle of July. She spent six weeks in the condemned cell, not knowing whether she was going to die or not—a hideous experience, a horribly refined torture which turned her hair quite white.

How much more fortunate was that other Charlotte, 142 years previously, sentenced and executed on the same day. If Charlotte Corday had spent six tortured weeks in the condemned cell, would she have faced death so bravely? Perhaps the French Revolutionaries were more humane than we are. They rejected with scorn the deputy who said that condemned prisoners should be bled white to sap their courage. But Charlotte Bryant was bled white before she was dragged, cringing and sobbing, to the gallows.

Meanwhile a desperate and dramatic fight was going on to save her life.

Immediately after the trial her counsel, Mr. J. D. Casswell, was startled to receive a letter from Professor W. A. Bone of the Imperial College of Science and Technology saying that he had a matter of great importance to discuss with him with reference to Dr. Roche Lynch's evidence in which he stated that coal ashes normally contain 40–50 parts per million arsenic, and that the ashes from the copper in the Bryants' house had 149 parts per million.

What Professor Bone had to say was sensational. Dr. Lynch's evidence about the normal proportion of arsenic in coal ashes was completely wrong. It was an established scientific fact that the normal content was *at least 140 parts per million* of arsenic and more likely to be a thousand to a million. Far from being high, the arsenical content of the boiler ashes in the Bryants' cottage was well below the average.

The effect of this was to refute the evidence of Mrs. Ostler, the Crown's chief witness on a very important point, and there was now no corroboration at all of her story about Charlotte's intention of getting rid of the weedkiller tin by burning it in the boiler. And so the defence lodged an appeal with every reason to suppose that it would be successful.

Professor Bone made a signed statement in direct contradiction of Dr. Lynch's evidence, and said he was prepared to give evidence before the Court of Criminal Appeal.

This court as a rule considers only the evidence given at the trial, but in the unusual circumstances which had now arisen, Mr. Casswell intimated in his written notice of appeal that he would ask the court in the interests of justice to hear what Professor Bone had to say.

The appeal was held on 10th July, and in the corridor outside the courtroom, the Solicitor General said to Mr. Casswell: "Lynch has certainly made a dreadful blunder. He knew nothing about the contents of coal ashes himself, but got his information over the telephone. He must have misheard what was said. It is quite obvious that he was wrong and you were right."*

After such an admission from the Crown, Charlotte's counsel faced the appeal judges with every confidence.

---

* Quoted in *A Lance For Liberty*, by J. D. Casswell, Q.C. (Harrap, 1961).

They received a rude shock. The Lord Chief Justice, Lord Hewart, had no patience with what he termed their "objectional application".

"This court will not listen to the opinion of scientific gentlemen bringing their minds to bear on evidence which they have not heard. This court sets its face like flint against attempts to call evidence which could have been made available at the trial." The Chief Justice added: "Moreover, in this case, it is clear that there has been no mistake."

The Solicitor General was not called upon to argue for the Crown and the appeal was summarily dismissed, much to the astonishment of everybody. Mr. Casswell's view is that the Solicitor General should have intervened and repeated what he had said in the corridor. But, thinks Mr. Casswell, he may have been too much taken aback to do so.

Mr. D. N. Pritt, K.C., then asked a question in the House. Would the Home Secretary consider introducing amending legislation to secure that verdicts founded on mistaken evidence should be subject to inquiry on appeal?

Sir John Simon replied: "I have ascertained from the Lord Chief Justice that he and the other judges sitting in the Court of Appeal proceeded on the assumption that this item of evidence was mistaken." Furthermore, he said, he had personally interviewed the trial judge, who had told him that in his view the matters put forward by Professor Bone did not affect in any way the validity of the jury's findings. In all the circumstances, even on the assumption that Dr. Roche Lynch had been wrong, the judges of the Court of Criminal Appeal had come to the conclusion that the other evidence of Mrs. Bryant's guilt was so strong that no miscarriage of justice had occurred. "And after the most careful examination," added Sir John, "I have reached the same view."

Was there any doubt of her guilt? The courts and the Home Office went into the facts pretty thoroughly and decided that there was not, and it would be unreasonable to hold that they were wrong.

What Charlotte's counsel says is not that she was innocent, but that if Dr. Lynch had not made that cardinal mistake the jury would very probably have returned a different verdict. She should not, therefore, have been hanged.

Mr. Casswell is very critical of the conduct of the Lord Chief Justice at the appeal and his tirade against the defence's efforts to bring before the appeal judges the evidence of "scientific gentlemen bringing their minds to bear on evidence which they have not heard."

After the appeal, Charlotte sent from her death cell a telegram to King Edward VIII:

Mighty King, have pity on your lowly and afflicted subject. Don't let them kill me on Wednesday.

This pathetic message, however, went to the Home Secretary, not to the King, who might have been more affected by it than Sir John Simon was. Sir John did not recommend a reprieve.

And so at eight o'clock on the morning of 15th July, 1936, the executioner, having for the past fifteen hours or so closely observed Charlotte through a secret spy-hole and worked out, from her age, weight and height, how much drop she required, came into her cell with his assistant, the prison governor, the chaplain and several male warders.

The executioner instantly pinioned the arms of the terrified Charlotte behind her back. The women warders who had been her constant companions on the death watch, left and were replaced by men, who half dragged the nearly fainting woman to the nearby execution chamber—preceded by the chaplain muttering the service for the dead.

Supported by two warders, her tottering feet were placed on the trap and swiftly lashed together. The executioner pulled a white hood from his pocket, flicked it open, and with a swift, practised movement, pulled it over Charlotte Bryant's now white hair and chalky, panic-stricken face. With another swift movement the executioner reached up, unhooked the coiled rope above the condemned woman's head, pulled the noose over the hooded face and secured the knot under the angle of the left jaw.

If he had placed the knot on the right-hand side, it would throw the head forward and strangle her. The knot on the left finishes up in front after the drop, throwing the chin back and breaking the spinal cord. In the event of a strangulation a hanged person could live for a quarter of an hour on the end of the rope. That was the hangman's theory, based on years of experience.

The knot secured swiftly under the left jaw, the hangman jumped quickly off the trap and instantly pulled the lever.

In the moment that elapsed between the second when the hands of the hangman left her and the deadly crack as the trap door opened, Charlotte swayed, and then suddenly dropped into the dark pit below, the rope spinning after her.

The rope jerked violently and was still. The chaplain stood close to the edge of the pit, eyes closed, lips moving.

In her will, Charlotte Bryant left 5s. 9½d. for her solicitor to divide among her five children, who, after their mother's execution, were adopted by the Dorset Public Assistance Committee.

Charlotte never admitted to the murder, though she did admit privately to her solicitor that it was she, not Mrs. Ostler, who had bought the weedkiller.

Valerie Storie
(1961)

IF THIS book needs a true heroine, here she is. Certainly Valerie Storie is a heroine in the etymological sense. She will go down in the history of crime as a brave and an avenging spirit.

What happened to her on that awful night of 22–3 August 1961 was enough to have broken most girls for life—mentally as well as physically. But not Valerie Storie. She not only survived appalling injuries, but she lived to avenge her lover who was murdered before her eyes, and is now taking up the threads of her life once more, paralysed from the waist down, but with a remarkable spirit of courage and confidence.

The public are used to horrors. Murders and rape constitute the staple diet of the majority of newspaper readers today. But the A6 murder, of which Valerie Storie and Michael Gregsten were the victims, sent a thrill of horror through the public such as it had rarely experienced before.

It was not the first time something like this had happened. But almost never before had a victim survived in such poignant and pitiful circumstances and been able to give a vivid and detailed account of the kind of thing that happens when a dangerous psychopath gets loose with a gun.

The bestial and purposeless crime for which James Hanratty was hanged was an imitation by a dangerous moron of what he had seen countless times at the cinema and on the telly. Clever actors playing brutal and homicidal psychopaths abound on the screen and the goggle-box. Is it any wonder that they have imitators among real homicidal psychopaths?

The man with the gun has absolute power in given circumstances. He can command absolute obedience, instil absolute terror, dispense death and suffering at will. This sort of scene is frequently described in fiction, but hardly ever taken to its logical conclusion. The gunman is usually stopped in time by the forces of law and order.

In real life it is different. The gunman is rarely stopped before he has pressed the trigger.

We know that Hanratty was a psychopath, who can be described as an individual who is emotionally unstable to an abnormal degree, though not suffering from a specific mental disorder. In 1952 he was diagnosed at St. Francis' Hospital, Haywards Heath, as a mental defective. This does not mean that he was mad or a lunatic in the accepted sense.

A mental defective is a person who is uneducatable, unable to maintain himself in anything but the simplest of environments. Such a person is a moron and is generally described as feeble-minded. There are many such people in society. Most of them are quite harmless, and many, under proper guidance, can be useful people who can lead happy lives. Such persons have moral responsibility, and know the difference between right and wrong.

Some people are uneasy about this case. Certainly Hanratty never confessed to it and pleaded his innocence right to the very end when it would not have made any difference what he said. Unlike Edith Thompson, Ruth Ellis, Derek Bentley, Timothy Evans and a number of other disturbing cases, the hanging of Hanratty was no propaganda for the abolitionists at the time. But when any body of disinterested people call into question the justice of an execution, it is time for society to take notice. The fact that a mistake like this can be made under the system of justice we practise in England is the greatest possible argument in favour of not bringing back the death penalty.

It is not my purpose here to discuss the guilt or otherwise of Hanratty. This chapter is about the young woman who identified him and accused him in open court of being the man who murdered her lover and then raped and shot her.

If you trace the events of the small hours of 23rd August in all their mad, terrifying reality, you can see how closely the murderer was imitating the gunman of the screen, whom he had seen and envied so often and whose actions he copied in every little detail, when at last he had a gun in his hand.

The fact that this was a purely imitative crime does not mean that the people who create gangster fiction, either in books or on the screen, are in any way responsible. I myself have written a great deal of crime fiction, though not of the sadistic kind involving rape and murder by which the A6 gunman seems to have been inspired.

It is as reasonable to blame the authors of this kind of fiction as it is to blame the makers of the gun which did the killing. If neither had existed, the A6 murderer would have committed some other crime equally as bestial.

It is just as profitless to try and imagine the world without make-believe gangsters as it is to imagine it without guns. They have to be accepted as part of civilisation. We shall never be without them.

Valerie Storie and Michael Gregsten were civil servants who worked for the Department of Scientific and Industrial Research at the Road Research Laboratory at Slough. At the time of the murder she was twenty-three. He was fourteen years older, a married man with two children.

Four years before the murder, they fell in love and had been having quite a serious affair. Valerie Storie herself stated this a few months after the trial in some articles she wrote in the magazine *Today*.

They both had a common interest, motor rallying, and frequently went off together on rallies. She introduced him to her parents, but did not tell them at first that he was married. She says Gregsten was in love with her, but was devoted to his children, so the problem created by their love affair was practically unsolvable. A common enough situation.

Later her parents found out that Gregsten was married, but though they must have been grieved about it, they still made him welcome in their home on the Cippenham Estate, Slough.

The car Gregsten and Valerie Storie used for their motor rallying was a Morris Minor, 847 BHN, which was owned jointly by Gregsten's mother and aunt, from whom Gregsten borrowed it.

On the evening of 22nd August, the two lovers met after work and went to the Stories' home at Slough, and then on to the Old Station Inn at Taplow, a pretty Thames-side village near Maidenhead. They were working on plans for an eighty-mile car rally through the Chiltern Hills for the motor club at the place where they worked.

Towards nine o'clock the pub started to fill up, and they left and drove to a place called Dorney Reach, not far away, and Gregsten stopped the car in a cornfield, parking it with its back to the road.

They had often been here before, leaving the car in the field and strolling down to the river to watch the boats go through the locks—a pleasant spot for lovers on a summer's evening.

But the evening of 22nd August 1961, was a chilly one, and they sat in the car with the windows up, still making plans for the rally. Valerie Storie says they were working out the system of penalty marks.

Just as it was getting dark there was a tap on the window at the driver's side. At first they were not alarmed, thinking perhaps it was someone from the farm wanting to drive a harvesting machine through the gateway.

Michael Gregsten wound down the window. They saw the figure of a man, neatly dressed, standing there, silhouetted against the darkening sky. The bottom half of his face was covered with a handkerchief. He poked a revolver through the window and said :

" This is a hold-up. I'm a desperate man. I've been on the run, so don't do anything silly."

At first Valerie Storie couldn't take it seriously. It was a stupid joke. The gun couldn't be real.

But Gregsten, closer to the gunman, instantly sensed this was no joke, and that they had a dangerous homicide on their hands.

The gunman demanded the car keys and told Gregsten to open the rear offside door. Gregsten obeyed and the intruder got in the back seat.

Both Gregsten and Valerie Storie were thoroughly scared by now and they had every reason to be. The man's attitude, particularly at first, warned them subconsciously how extremely dangerous he was.

The armed gunman of fiction nearly always has a purpose. He is anxious to execute a criminal exploit, or get away from one. His gun gives him power to force people to assist him in these ends. If the people he holds up do not try to foil him, generally speaking they don't get shot.

But the gunman *without* a purpose is another matter, and is infinitely more dangerous.

The man who held up Gregsten and Valerie Storie was the gunman without a purpose. That was obvious as soon as he got into the car. He had held up two people with a gun, and then he didn't know what to do about it—apart from shooting them.

Gregsten and Valerie Storie were doomed from the start. It is only by a mixture of good fortune and an indomitable courage that she is alive today, and that this dreadful story is able to be told.

The moment he got in the car, the gunman betrayed the childlike mind of the moron at work. (" Be quiet, will you—I am finking "). He in fact behaved exactly as would the mental defective certified at St. Francis Hospital in 1952.

Just before his execution the *Observer* published medical records which disclosed Hanratty's mental state. The *Observer* was hotly criticised by Hanratty's solicitors for doing so.

Hanratty's defence had always been, and was to the end, that he did not do it. He wasn't the man. But the identification of him was positive enough to convince a jury. The medical documents later published by the *Observer* provide further evidence of identification.

The actions of the armed man who got into the back of Gregsten's car on the evening of 22nd August were not inconsistent with the mentality of the man who was diagnosed as a mental defective in St. Francis Hospital nine years previously. But they are not proof, of course. There are many thousands of mental defectives.

Consider how the gunman acted when he first got these two people at his mercy. He was completely without purpose. Having perpetrated the initial outrage of holding them up with the gun, he did not know what to do next. They offered him the car, their money, their watches. They would have done anything to have got rid of him. But he would not let them go. What did he want? The girl's body? Or just to cling on to the power the gun gave him? Both perhaps, though his lust for the girl was not apparent till later, till he had shot Gregsten. For undoubtedly killing Gregsten excited him sexually—a not uncommon psychopathic condition.

So at first they sat in the car for two wretched hours in that field. The gunman said he hadn't eaten for two days and had slept rough, which was obviously untrue. He kept looking at his watch, saying there was plenty of time, but obviously he was not clear what there was plenty of time for.

The nightmare of the next few hours as told later by Valerie Storie is probably without parallel in the annals of human experience. People who suffer such appalling inhumanities at the hands of their fellow men are rarely able to give a vivid and detailed account of their sufferings.

The remarkable thing about this case was that when Valerie Storie recovered consciousness in hospital the next day her mind was as clear as a bell, despite the awful injuries she had received. She could remember every tiny detail of what she and Gregsten suffered.

The gunman sat in the back of the car, brandishing the revolver and his conversation gave an ominous indication of his mentality and intentions.

" This is like a cowboy's gun. I feel like a cowboy. I haven't had it very long. I have never shot anyone before."

He made Gregsten drive farther into the field and then demanded their watches and money. Gregsten gave him his wallet containing about three pounds. Valerie Storie took seven pounds out of her handbag before she gave the gunman the bag, secreting the money inside her bra.

He told them that every policeman in England was looking for him, and that he intended to wait till morning, tie them up, take the car and leave.

About 10.30 a light came on in a nearby house and a man came out to put his bicycle away. This made the gunman nervous and he told his victims that if the man should come up to the car, they must say nothing, or he would shoot the man and them also.

Another nerve-racking hour passed with the couple in the front seats trying everything they knew to persuade him to go away and leave them.

At 11.30 the gunman grew nervous. He forced Gregsten at gunpoint to drive out of the field and take the road to Slough.

Valerie Storie said that now she noticed an edge to Michael Gregsten's voice which told her how near to breaking point he was. As they continued their ghastly ride the two in front continually touched hands to try and comfort and reassure each other. It seems that Valerie Storie was the calmest of the three.

They went through Slough where she noticed that a clock showed a quarter-to-twelve. Behind them as they drove at gunpoint, they heard a clicking noise. The gunman told them that he was putting the safety catch on and off. They were forbidden to look around in case they should see his face in the passing lights.

Near London Airport they stopped at a garage for petrol. The gunman was as precise in his instructions as they are in such circumstances on the screen.

" I want you to get two gallons. You are to stay in the car. I have the gun pointing at you and if you try to say anything else than to ask for two gallons, or give the man a note, or make any indication that anything is wrong, then I will shoot you."

He gave Gregsten one pound of the money he had previously taken from him and Gregsten did as he was told. The unsuspecting attendant put in the petrol and gave him 10s. 3d. change.

The gunman took the ten-shilling note and gave Valerie Storie the threepence, saying: "You can have that as a wedding present." He insisted on believing that she and Gregsten were married, although they told him several times that they were not.

They then drove on, through Hayes and Harrow and across North-west London.

In Stanmore they stopped while Gregsten got out and got some cigarettes from a machine, the gunman holding the girl as a hostage in the car.

No doubt Gregsten hoped he might be able to summon assistance in some way, but there was nobody about, and nothing he could do, with this unpredictable gunman holding Valerie at his mercy. Their captor, whoever he was, had learnt his part well.

So the unhappy Gregsten returned to the car with the cigarettes, not dreaming of running away suddenly and deserting the girl he loved—as he undoubtedly could have done just then. And later, when her opportunity came to make a break for it, she refused to desert him. Afraid they undoubtedly were, but they showed great loyalty as well as courage on this awful night.

And so they drove on.

Valerie Storie lit two cigarettes, giving one to Gregsten, handing the other into the back for their captor to take. She noticed he was wearing black gloves. Although the gunman took the cigarette, he said he did not like smoking—a further known characteristic of Hanratty's.

They turned on to the A5, and Gregsten tried again to attract attention. He kept switching the reversing light on and off. A passing driver turned and pointed.

At this, the gunman exclaimed: "They must know something is wrong." He made Gregsten stop and get out with him to examine the rear lights.

While they were doing this, Valerie Storie, herself a good driver, could easily have slipped into the driving seat and driven off and saved herself from the appalling thing that was done to her. But this extraordinarily brave girl could not bring herself to abandon the man she loved.

178

Who knows what would have happened if she had made a break for it at this point? The nervous, indecisive gunman would almost certainly have fired at the car, and only a very lucky shot could have hit the driver. Gregsten, if he had been quick enough, might have made a successful dive for the gun at the moment when the gunman's attention was distracted, and the story might have had a very different ending.

But the gunman had assured them that he would not harm them so long as they did as he told them, and Valerie Storie decided not to take a risk which would undoubtedly have provoked him to violence.

Besides, Gregsten scorned to desert her. So she scorned to desert him.

They got into the car again and Gregsten drove on to his death. But he still tried to attract the attention of passing cars by switching the reversing light on and off and flashing the headlamps from dipped beam to main beam.

"Every time we entered a built-up area we went slowly," said Valerie Storie. "And we had a plan that if we managed to see a policeman Mike would pretend there was something wrong with the steering and try to run the car on the pavement near a policeman. But there was no policeman. You never see one when you want one." They did not see one policeman during the whole of this terrible journey.

And so they went to St. Albans and on to the A6—the road that goes from London to Leicester, Derby, Manchester and Carlisle.

The gunman said he was tired and said: "I want a kip." He told Gregsten to turn off the road and find somewhere where he could sleep. Twice they parked but found out they were on private property, so they went on.

Finally they came to a place known as Dead Man's Hill, where there was a layby which was separated from the road by a grass verge on which were some trees. Here the gunman made Gregston turn in and park, with the car pointing in the direction of Luton and turn all the lights out.

Again they begged him not to shoot them. He said if he had wanted to do that, he would have done so before.

" I want a kip," he said. " But first I must tie you up."

He made Gregsten get out of the car, go round to the boot with him where he found a piece of cord which he gave to Gregsten and told him to get back into the driver's seat. Then he tied Valerie Storie's hands behind her and fastened them to the car door handle, but she managed to keep her wrists apart so that she could easily get them free when she wanted to.

The gunman then looked for something to tie Gregsten with. He decided to use the cord from the duffel bag containing some clean laundry.

The story of what happened then is best told in the girl's own words, at the trial.

" Somehow the duffel bag had got into the front of the car. The man said ' Give me that bag up '. Mike picked up the bag with both hands, turned towards the interior of the car to his left. He lifted the bag and as the bag was just about to go over the back of the seat, the man fired two shots in quick succession at Mike's head. The gun could not have been more than an inch or two from his head. There was a terrific noise and a smell of gunpowder.

" Mike fell forward and over the steering wheel and I could hear the blood pouring out of his head.

" For the first time that night, I screamed.

" Hanratty said : ' Stop screaming ! '

" I turned to him and said : ' You shot him, you bastard ! Why did you do that ?"

" He said : ' He frightened me. He moved too quick. I got frightened.'

" My hands by this time were free of the rope and I was holding them together as if they were secure. Mike moved and flopped back against the seat. His head fell back. There was a look of surprise, disbelief in his face.

" I said to the man : ' For God's sake let me get Mike to a doctor quick. I will do anything you want if you will let me take the car and get Mike to a doctor.'

" He said : ' Be quiet, I am finking.'

" I said : ' Let me move Mike. I will take the car. I will

180

take you anywhere you want to go. Let me drive and find help for Mike.'

" He said : ' No, he's dead.'

" I said : ' Let me take Mike somewhere. I must try and get help.'

" He said : ' Be quiet, will you? I am finking.' Then : ' Turn round and face me. I know your hands are free.'

" I obeyed.

" He looked at me. ' Kiss me.'

" I refused.

" While we were in this position facing each other, a car came from the direction of Luton towards Bedford lighting up the man's face. This was my first opportunity of really seeing what he looked like. He had very large, pale-blue staring icy eyes. He seemed to have a pale face. I should imagine anyone would have, having just shot someone. He had brown hair, combed back, no parting.

" He said again : ' Kiss me.' I refused, and after he had asked several times, he pointed the gun at me and said : ' If you don't, I will count five and I will shoot you.'

" I said : ' Please don't shoot me. Just let me go.' And he started to count, so I let him kiss me very briefly.

" After that had happened, I sat back in the car. The gun was in his right hand as it had been the whole evening. I leaned across with my left hand and tried to grab the gun, but he was too strong.

" He said : ' That was a silly thing to do. I thought you were sensible. I cannot trust you now '."

He took a cloth from the duffel bag and covered the dead man's face with it. Gregsten's body was slumped in the driving seat, his blood flowing down between the seat and the side of the car.

She continues:

" He said : ' Come and sit in the back with me.' I said : ' No.' Several times he asked me and several times I refused. He said : ' Get out. Come and sit in the back with me. I will count five and if you have not got in, I will shoot.'

" I got out of the car slowly, trying to play for time, hoping

181

someone would come by. He was sitting in the car and opened the rear door for me, with the gun on me pointing at me all the time.

"He said: 'Come on, get in.' Again I refused. So he got out of the car and the gun was almost touching me, and he said: 'Come on—get in.' I got in the back. He followed and shut the door.

"The gun was resting on his lap. He tried to kiss me again. He tried to touch me. I managed to remove the seven pounds from my bra into my macintosh pocket. He put the gun on the back window shelf of the car and took off one of his black gloves."

Then he made her undo her brassiere, mauled her, and made her take off her knickers and lie back in the car while he undid his trousers and raped her.

"This lasted," said Valerie Storie, "only a very short time— a minute or so. He said: 'You haven't had much sex, have you?'"

She said afterwards that the rape itself seemed unimportant. The only thing she was thinking of was Gregsten, slumped there just in front of them, still bleeding.

The murderer then made her pull Gregsten's body out of the car, which she did by grasping him under the armpits. She dragged it round the back of the car to the edge of the concrete strip two or three yards behind the car. He made no attempt to help her, and was careful not to get any blood on himself.

He carefully wiped the steering wheel and covered up the bloodstained driving seat and made her start the engine and show him how the controls worked.

She went and sat beside Gregsten's body, her legs under her, her back to the car. She said she did not weep, but just sat there waiting for the murderer to go.

Minutes passed. He was still undecided whether to leave her, or to commit further outrage. He had already got into the car more than once.

She continues the story:

"He got out and came up to me and said: 'I think I had

better hit you on the head or get something to knock you out, or you will go for help.'

" I said: ' No, I won't. I won't move. Just go.' I gave him £1 from my pocket. ' Here you are. You can have that if you will go quick.' He said: ' Where did you get that from?' I said it was just in my pocket. He took the pound and started to walk away.

" When he was about six or ten feet away he suddenly turned round and started to shoot. I felt one bullet hit me, then a second. I felt the use of my legs go and I fell over."

One of the bullets had gone straight through her neck close to the spinal cord.

" He fired another two or three shots at me while I was lying on the ground. There was a pause and I heard a clicking as if he was reloading. Then he fired another three shots and they seemed to go over my head.

" I lay perfectly still. I heard him walk towards me, and I tried to stop breathing and pretend I was dead. I felt him touch me. Whether it was with his hand or whether he kicked me, I do not know. He stood looking at me for a few seconds."

Valerie Storie says in retrospect that this was the most terrifying moment of all.

Then he went away.

" I heard him walk back to the car, get in, slam the door, saw him put on the headlights. He drove off in the direction of Luton.

" I managed to turn over on to my back and thought what do I do now? I found I could not move. I thought of trying to roll along the layby and get on the road, but I could not move. I thought to myself, If I die now, no one will know who to look for, and with my right hand I tried to get up some little stones and I was trying to make out the words: Blue eyes, brown hair. But there were not any stones.

" I must have been lying there for almost half an hour when I heard a vehicle approach. As it got nearer I started to scream and shout for help. It just went by."

She managed to pull off her petticoat and tried to wave it to attract attention.

It was now about three o'clock, some six hours after that tap on the car window in the cornfield at Dorney Reach. She presently lost consciousness.

"When next I opened my eyes it was light. I looked back and on the verge behind me, I saw a pair of legs, and I shouted for help."

The man who found her was a young undergraduate engaged on a traffic census. He soon summoned help and before she was taken to hospital she was able to give a brief description of the murderer.

For six terrible hours he had sat behind her in the car talking, and it was natural that it was his voice which was indelibly imprinted on her mind—quietly spoken, youngish and Cockney, unable to pronounce " th ". Thus " things " were " fings " and " thinking " was " finking ". This as much as anything put the noose around Hanratty's neck.

Valerie Storie woke up in hospital with the doctors bending anxiously over her and the police in the background not having much hope that a girl who had been so savaged and outraged would be coherent enough to help them much in their urgent inquiries—even if she could bear to talk about it.

But they were soon to discover this was no ordinary girl they were dealing with. By some remarkable fortune, her mind was crystal clear on every detail of her terrible experience. Despite her pain and her helplessness, a cold rage was burning inside her. One thought was uppermost in her mind—she wanted to avenge her lover's death. In those long weeks in hospital, through the nightmares and the suffering, she thought of little else.

The A6 murderer in that mad senseless night had smashed more than two lives. There was Gregsten's widow, left in an appalling situation with two fatherless children.

There were many who criticised Valerie Storie as she lay in hospital paralysed, with an irreparable injury to her spinal column. Some even wrote poison-pen letters to her, telling her she was a wicked woman who had got what she deserved and that she had wrecked a good man's life.

Anonymous phone calls were made to the hospital threatening her life. She was guarded night and day by police and dogs. Every night her bed was moved to a different position in case someone should try and shoot her through the window to silence her.

Who threatened her life? We shall never know. Hanratty denied everything to the end. It was most likely the act of deranged individuals who are called, for the want of better words, practical jokers.

Not only did the police guard her carefully, they also did their best to spare her feelings when questioning her by glossing over the more unpleasant details of that night of horror. But they were surprised to find that she was not to be hurried over her awful tale, and was meticulous in describing every little detail of what had happened.

Her calm, matter-of-fact attitude helped the police enormously in their inquiries.

For her part she found them " so patient, so understanding, so untiring and so human ".

As she lay in hospital, through all the pain and suffering she said she had only one thought—revenge. She knew no pity for the murderer. She wanted him to be hanged for what he had done.

In October, barely two months after the outrage, she picked Hanratty out at an identification parade. Later he was identified by someone else in connection with the case and charged. Early the following year his trial took place—the longest and one of the most controversial murder trials in English history.

One of the controversies centred around the fact that in September, Valerie Storie picked out a different man at another identification parade—someone who had obviously nothing to do with the crime. She had plainly made a mistake, and this, of course, was held against the validity of her later evidence. She picked out Hanratty at a second identification parade.

At this second parade each of the men was asked to say, " Be quiet, will you? I am thinking." At the first parade the men said nothing. It was hearing Hanratty speak these words—he had said them so many times during the night of the murder— that clinched it in her mind.

Upon the identification of the accused man by Valerie Storie the prosecution's case rested. Without it, there would have been no conviction. The defence were unable to shake her evidence in court and the jury believed her.

The trial of James Hanratty at Bedford Assizes began on 22nd January 1962, and lasted until 17th February. It was the longest murder trial in British legal history.

The judge was Mr. Justice Gorman and there was a jury of eleven men. The Crown was led by Mr. Graham Swannick, Q.C., and Hanratty's counsel was Mr. Michael Sherrard, who was then a junior member of the Bar. Although opinion is that Mr. Sherrard defended Hanratty very well, he was not a Q.C., and some legal authorities have said that a person on a capital charge should always have leading counsel to defend him as well as a junior.

No question of expense enters into this. When Hanratty was committed for trial, the magistrates at Ampthill authorised him legal aid which could have provided him with both senior and junior counsel, as is usual in capital charges.

Hanratty, however, had implicit faith in Mr. Sherrard's ability to save him from the gallows, and insisted that he should conduct his defence without the benefit of senior counsel. Hanratty was entitled to make this vital decision, regardless of whether he was mentally equipped to do so. It was up to him also to decide what plea he should make. He had the benefit of legal advice, of course, but the decision was his to make. He pleaded not guilty—a total denial. He maintained he wasn't the man, and said he was somewhere else at the time. This sounds like the decision of a reasonably intelligent, if cunning person, and Hanratty certainly gave that impression in the witness box. He was cocky, even insolent.

However restrained he was in the courtroom, outside he was less reticent. While in Brixton Prison he boasted to a fellow prisoner that he was the A6 killer.

As the crime was on everyone's lips just then, too much evidence need not necessarily have been placed upon such a boast by a psychopath with delusions of criminal grandeur. But, it was said, Hanratty confided details of the crime which, at that time, only Valerie Storie, the police and the killer knew. He must therefore have been the killer.

This came out only in part at the trial. Owing to the peculiar nature of English courtroom procedure, which often acts very largely in the accused's favour, the whole story of the A6 killing and the circumstances surrounding it could not be told.

The whole story indeed has never been told, and may never be. But this particular piece of evidence against Hanratty, though not known to the court, was known to the Home Secretary when he was considering the question of a reprieve, and may well have sealed Hanratty's fate.

Over a million words of evidence were spoken at this marathon of a trial. There were moments of drama among the long hours of weighty argument and apparently inconsequential testimony.

The high moment of the trial, of course, was the appearance of Valerie Storie to give her evidence, brightly dressed in tartan slacks and yellow sweater and seated in a wheelchair. No one who saw and heard her could fail to be touched to the heart. She gave her evidence simply but with great conviction, and, of course, was handled with kid gloves by cross-examining counsel.

We have heard the story she told. The legal pundits don't give much credence to her evidence owing to the identification problem.

An important and contentious point was brought up by the defence, when it alleged that the police investigations were directed not so much at finding out the truth but at discovering things which would implicate Hanratty.

This is not unusual in police practice. If the police suspect a person, their lines of inquiry are directed at discovering evidence against him. This is not necessarily unfair, nor could it be called disregarding the truth. If the facts the police uncover suggest that their suspect is innocent, then obviously they are not going to waste time on an investigation which is not going to result in a *prima facie* case.

The police were severely criticised by the defence particularly on their investigation into Hanratty's alibis, but as these alibis apparently turned out to be false and were abandoned by the defence, much of the criticism, though it sounded formidable enough at the time, did not really amount to much when the case was considered in retrospect. It is true that the police were deliberately selective in their lines of investigation, but they were fully entitled to be, once having decided that Hanratty was their man.

One of the unsolved mysteries of the case was Hanratty's relationship with a man called Charles France.

France and his family lived in St. John's Wood and Hanratty had been staying there about the time of the A6 murder. France gave evidence for the prosecution to the effect that he was riding on a bus with Hanratty, who asked him whether the back seat of the top of a bus was a good place to hide a gun. This was just where the murder weapon was later found.

France himself was a mental case and suffered from acute depression. He had always lived on the fringe of the underworld and undoubtedly knew of Hanratty's criminal aspirations.

His association with Hanratty worsened France's mental condition and three days before the trial he tried to commit suicide. Under psychiatric treatment France revealed that he was acutely worried about the great harm he had done his family by introducing Hanratty into his home. " It could have been my wife and daughter that he killed." France had an overwhelming guilt complex about the A6 murder.

A month after the trial ended and less than three weeks before Hanratty's execution, France finally succeeded in committing suicide, leaving letters expressing great bitterness towards Hanratty.

The inquest on him was adjourned until after Hanratty's execution on 4th April, 1962, because the disclosure might, the coroner thought, prejudice Hanratty's chances of a reprieve.

When he did hold the inquest the coroner refused to read the whole of the suicide letter, saying : " The rest of the letter I think is not in the public interest to read, but he explains that he had an association with a man, James Hanratty, and having been a witness at the trial of that man had played on his mind very much. He blames himself very much for having introduced the man to his family at all. It is a letter written with great bitterness and great feeling."

What was the mystery of their relationship? The *Observer* said : " If Mr. Butler is the man of integrity we believe him to be he will make a public statement which fills in the gaps of the story of the A6 murder. The community has a right to know."

But the Home Secretary remained silent.

The letters mentioned by the coroner were shown to Hanratty's solicitor, but whatever they contained, they did nothing to bring about a reprieve for Hanratty.

From his death cell Hanratty wrote : " I can't say how sorry I am that things turned out this way, but it was not my fault. It was the fault of others. I am about to take the punishment for someone else's crime, but I will face it like a man."

The final unanswered question is what was Hanratty doing in that lonely cornfield in Buckinghamshire that August evening with a gun in his hand? He was miles away from his usual haunts. What was he doing at Dorney Reach?

The mysteries of the A6 murder case will perhaps never be solved. Criminologists will discuss it for years to come.

Let Valerie Storie, who because of it is fated to spend the rest of her life in a wheelchair, have the last word : " We all do things in life which we should not do. Sometimes we escape unhurt. Sometimes we pay the price for it. For those who escape we say they are the lucky ones."

THE END